ANSWERING GOD'S CALL:

Reflections of a Veteran Missionary in Asia

Foreword by Bill Snider

Published by
Sambayanihan Publishers
Duplex 2A APTS
444 Ambuklao Rd.
Baguio City, 2600
Philippines
Moblie No: 09774267631
EMAIL: sambayanihan@gmail.com

All rights to distribution and marketing
have been licensed to:
Asia Pacific Theological Seminary Press
444 Ambuklao Rd.
Baguio City, 2600
Philippines
(074) 442 6977 loc 331
EMAIL: apts.press@apts.edu

Printed in the Philippines

Cover design and layout by *Mil Santos* (milsantos.apts@gmail.com)

ISBN 978-621-8255-04-3 (Paperback)
        978-621-8255-05-0 (Mobi/Kindle)
        978-621-8255-06-7 (EPUB)

Table of Contents

Foreword

By William Snider

Writing is a discipline. That's why not many take up the pen, or today, sit for hours before a keyboard to write a story. Writing is not easy and requires reflection, honesty and truth telling.

I've always enjoyed missionary stories, biographies, or memoirs. In my coming to follow God's call to missions, he used missionary stories and a biography to fan the flame of calling.

Dave Johnson has produced a life memoir that illustrates God's grace and his leading. I've known Dave for over 30 years, and have appreciated his heart for evangelism, for service, and his diligence in pursuing a call that would leave a legacy. He's been intentional and looked at ministry through the lens of multiplying the Message. From evangelistic meetings, to mentoring, to pursuing advanced studies and now through a passion that Asian theologians and leaders would write and influence their church and the next generations, Dave has passionately pursued the call. He and Debbie are pursuing a life that is invested in Kingdom purposes.

As in most stories, you may find links to your own life. I think you will be encouraged to see how God worked in the life of one man, walking with him through times of joy and times of struggle. From this story, we can reaffirm how God will work in each of our lives. Dave has provided detail, not glossed over times of searching, and in that has provided an encouraging word that affirms our God who does all things well.

In this memoir you will find many names of colleagues and co-workers mentioned. We will see how God uses people to encourage us, challenge us and guide our steps. Our lives are intertwined, and God guides through relationships.

May this book bless and encourage a future generation of workers in the ways of God and the faithfulness of God, that we may all leave a legacy.

Acknowledgments

To Jesus, without whom I have nothing to offer anyone. To Debbie, my wife, soulmate and best friend, for nearly twenty-four years of wonderful marriage. To my parents, Arnie and Marion Johnson, my two brothers, Steve and Tom, to Joyce, my stepmother and Kristie, my stepsister, who mean so much to me.

To Richard Dresselhaus, Roy Sapp, Ernest Oliver, M. Wayne Benson, and to a small legion of coaches, teachers, counselors, pastors, mentors and others, who have mentored and molded me in one way or another.

To all of my professors and mentors at Central Bible College, the Assemblies of God Theological Seminary and the Asia Graduate School of Theology. To Drs. W. Charles Harris and the late Dr. Jesse Moon,

To my missionary colleagues, past and present, our supporting churches and innumerable friends all over the globe, of whom there are far too many to even try to name. If you don't already know how special you are, you know it now.

Dedication

To all of our sons and daughters in the faith,
wherever in the world you may be.

Introduction

Let me make something clear from the beginning. Writing my memoirs does not mean that we are retiring. Far from it. We intend to be in missions for as long as God wants us here.

This book is about leaving a legacy, hopefully a good one. In every one of my personal journals I write these thoughts on the first page, "Live, love, laugh, learn, lament, leave a legacy worth following." I have tried my best to do this here, but you can be the judge of whether I have succeeded.

Why do it now? Most people think about leaving a legacy for their children and grandchildren. The problem for Debbie and me is that we do not have any biological children. But we do have a lot of spiritual children, those whose lives we have touched for Christ in some way over the years. Since most of those spiritual children are in Asia, especially the Philippines, I wanted to write this memoir now while we are still here to help get this book into the hands of as many as possible.

In this book I have done my best to trace the major events, both good and otherwise, and describe the people that God has used to shape my life and made me into the person that I am. Since the people God has used most in my life are my parents, I will start at the beginning and try to trace the things that they taught me in my growing up years, through my time in the Navy, the years of theological education afterward, and the more than three decades of ministry that have followed. Along the way I have been mentored by a small legion of pastors, Bible college and seminary professors, other leaders and authors beyond number. In many respects, I am what I am today because of them.

Most of the book is in chronological order. However, since we have been involved in many ministries simultaneously in our years in missions, I do not always follow a strict chronological order in those chapters. I found it necessary to weave back and forth chronologically in those chapters in order to present each ministry in a coherent manner.

Over the years, my life has been touched and enhanced by more family members, pastors, Bible school and seminary professors, friends and colleagues than I can possibly name here. For those unnamed, I beg your forgiveness. Please know that I have not forgotten you.

As you read these chapters, my prayer is that you will not only find hope and inspiration from what God has done in my life, but that you might also learn some lessons from the mistakes I have made. Furthermore, I pray that you will consider the question as to what kind of legacy you will leave behind. Finally, I hope you think about how you might equip those who follow you, be it your own children, grandchildren, family, friends, or others, to serve the purposes of God in their generation (Acts 13:36).

I welcome your comments. You can reach me by email at dave.johnson@agmd.org.

Dave Johnson
Asia Pacific Theological Seminary
Baguio City, Philippines
December 15, 2020

CHAPTER 1
My Early Years

I was rather surprised one day to realize that not everybody saw the world through the eyes of a white, middle class, suburban American male. My ignorance came largely from the fact that, like anybody else, I was a product of my environment. Everyone in my church, neighborhood and high school, with one exception, was as "lily white" as I was. I am relieved to say that much has changed over the years, and I am a better man for it. But before I get into that story, I need to explain my background, focusing on the people, traditions and events that have shaped my life.

I was born during a thunderstorm on April 3, 1957, in Grand Rapids, Michigan. That thunderstorm may have prophetically declared certain elements of my character! My parents, Arnold and Marion Johnson, had three boys. Steve was born in 1956, just ten and a half months before me. I was well into adulthood before I realized that my poor mother had only about six weeks between pregnancies! My parents had always wanted at least one girl, but God had other plans, and Tom, the youngest, arrived in January, 1961. They accepted it as God's will, but they sure were happy when we all eventually married and they could have daughters-in-law!

Grand Rapids was, and to a great degree continues to be, a safe, conservative, and traditional community, where many families put down deep roots. Together with the neighboring town of Holland, it is also the largest enclave in America of those with a Dutch heritage, and we were no exception. When my paternal great-grandfather immigrated to

Grand Rapids, his last name was Jansen. According to family lore, he changed it to Johnson, which is Scandinavian, because he thought it sounded more American. My mother's side of the family was also Dutch. One of my great-grandmothers was well-remembered for loving to read her Dutch Bible. All my grandparents, however, were born in America, and to the best of my knowledge, did not learn the Dutch language, although they all were proud of their heritage. The common joke around Grand Rapids was, "if you're not Dutch, you're not much," although I suspect that those who were not Dutch might not have thought it funny.

While my grandparents were temporarily living out of the area when my dad was born, both of my parents grew up within an hour's drive of Grand Rapids. Except for my dad's two-year stint in the Army during the Korean war, they lived their entire lives in the Grand Rapids area, as did most of our extended family. Many of their aunts, uncles and cousins did the same. Since my dad's mother came from a family of eight children who all settled in southwestern Michigan, where Grand Rapids is located, he had a lot of family in the area. With the birth of my nephew's first son in 2016, the sixth generation of our family began life there. While I have lived most of my adult life elsewhere, I still feel a deep rootedness whenever I return there.

My earliest memories are of family, church, school and sports. My parents were both raised in the Christian Reformed Church (CRC), which in my youth was mainly made up of Dutch families, and they saw no reason to change when they got married and had a family. We went to church every Sunday morning and every Sunday night. In American churches, it is common for the church to provide a nursery, a room where parents can deposit their children with caregivers while they attend the worship service. My parents, however, believed that children belonged in the sanctuary. There was no playing in the nursery for us.

Church in that day was a rather formal affair that called for wearing our best clothes. From a young age, women were expected to wear either dresses or skirts and blouses and males were expected to wear a suit and tie. I think my brothers and I were introduced into this tradition at about the age of three! I remember being horrified once to see a non-conformist teenager attend a service in blue jeans!

There was never any doubt about what our Sunday activities would be. Sunday School, church services, and later, youth group activities, were a normal part of our lives. Our church frowned on watching TV, listening to the radio and doing a number of other things on Sunday. For example, playing catch with a glove and ball was allowed, but getting out a baseball bat was considered sinful. While it was an honest effort to "keep the Sabbath day holy," my parents eventually realized that the law of God and the traditions of the church were not necessarily the same thing and relaxed their views. But the positive value of these restrictions reinforced the truth that Sunday was indeed a special day, a value I have carried throughout my life.

Relaxing these standards, however, brought some other challenges, particularly for my mother. Mom loved to play the piano, which she did marvelously, and she loved to sing the great hymns of the church. Since we did not watch television on Sunday, she would often fill those afternoon hours on the piano, which was in the dining room directly adjacent to the living room. Once Dad started watching sports on Sunday afternoons, however, Mom could not play the piano as much, and this would occasionally lead to vocal complaints, and ultimately a compromise! To this day, no genre of music resonates so deeply in my spirit as the great hymns that I learned in church and from my mother.

My dad would normally read a chapter of the Bible at night after supper. He would often stop without warning and ask one of us kids what was the last word he had read. My dad normally gave a stern lecture about the merits of listening to the Word of God to any child caught not paying attention. My parents also believed in Christian education and sent us to Christian schools for as long as they could afford it which, for me, meant through the fifth grade. They were also strong disciplinarians, believing that sparing the rod would spoil their children. My mother used a paddle, but for my dad, who did manual labor all his life, the strength of his right hand was sufficient in administering justice. One on occasion, I misbehaved while sitting in church. Normally, my parents would wait until we got home to deal with us so as not to embarrass us, but on this occasion, I must have really irritated Dad because he hauled me out of the sanctuary by the arm in the middle of the pastor's sermon, took me downstairs where he gave me a good spanking, and returned me to the pew while the minister was still speaking! I do not recall anyone mentioning anything afterward. Probably every kid in church had experienced the same thing at one time or another. I should also note that the spanking and public shaming did indeed correct my misbehavior.

Given the current social climate in America, I want to state emphatically that my parents were never abusive and I do not think that we were necessarily spanked more than any other child in our generation. My parents had a clear sense of right and wrong and sought to instill it in us. They did not do it perfectly, but as I reflect on my childhood now, they were consistent in what they punished us for and what they did not. They were also consistent in treating all three of us equally.

In 1965, just before my eighth birthday, we moved out of Grand Rapids to a suburb called Wyoming (not to be confused with the American state by the same name). We were part of what sociologists would later call "white flight," when much of the white population fled the inner cities to the suburbs as part of the post-World War II building boom in the 1950s and 60s. In our case, the house that we had been renting in Grand Rapids was sold out from underneath us and we had no choice but to move. For my parents, it was the first home they had ever owned and they were thrilled.

We also changed churches, since there was a Christian Reformed Church within walking distance of our new house. The house had an open side lot, which either served as a playground, vegetable garden, baseball field, or all the above. When Dad saw that I had picked out one side of the garage for a place to throw the rubber ball that I used in place of a baseball, he gave up and boarded up the window on that side of the garage, knowing that I would surely break it if he did not. He then put up another board with a home plate drawn on it so I could practice my pitching—which I did by the hour. He also put up a basketball rim and backboard on the front of the garage, and was always willing to move the car whenever we wanted to play.

From my earliest memories, my dad has been a Detroit Tigers baseball fan. I was hooked for life, long before he took me to me to see my first game at the tender age of nine. I played baseball in Little League until age 12, and then sporadically through the end of my freshman year of high school. I have often told people that I grew up with the Bible in one hand and a baseball glove on the other. To this day, we all remain Tigers' fans and I follow them over the internet from the other side of the world!

One of the greatest memories I have of my childhood is that Dad would play ball with us and almost always attended my ballgames, whether baseball, football or basketball—with Mom right there with him. I do not ever recall them having interests or hobbies outside of home, work and church at least until Steve and I were out of high school.

My brothers and I have gotten along well all our lives. But my parents did tell me that if there was a fight, it was normally me and one of my brothers or all three of us. They said I was normally the instigator. One day, Steve was riding our rocking horse[1] and I decided it was my turn. Rather than waiting for him to finish, I simply pushed him off. Steve screamed and Mom intervened. My ride came to a swift, unhappy ending and Mom made me apologize. Clearly, my choleric nature was already on display. It would not be the only time that I pushed or steam rolled over someone to achieve my goal. One Filipino pastor would later tell a

---

[1] A rocking horse is a toy horse on springs that is big enough for small children to ride.

fellow missionary that I was good at apologizing, but that was only because I have had lots of opportunities to practice.

Somewhere along the line someone, probably my parents, introduced me to the Hardy Boys detective books for boys, and I have loved books ever since. Mom also loved to read and I think this contributed to my becoming a first-rate "bookworm," a habit I have carried through life.

My memories of going to Christian schools are quite pleasant. One school, which I attended for three years, had a large playground that had a small wooded area, an ideal place for boys to build "forts" and other such manly things, and where girls were not welcome. The woods also had a creek running through them, and on more than one occasion, I went home with wet shoes and socks, something my mother somehow failed to appreciate. We rode the bus to and from school. I can remember my brothers and I standing by the bus stop on cold, winter mornings before the sun came up, waiting for the bus.

Since the same bus had to run two routes, we sometimes had to wait at the school when it was our turn to be on the second route for the trip home. On one occasion, I played in the woods while waiting for the bus and stayed out too long. I returned to the schoolyard to see the bus returning from its final run, meaning that I had missed it and would get home later. Fortunately, the bus driver lived on our street and took me home to a rather unhappy mother!

When I started the sixth grade, we had to switch to the public school because my parents could no longer afford the Christian school. Since my classmates were from the same neighborhood and I already knew them, the change was not hard. While most of my childhood memories are positive and heartwarming, this time would also see the beginning of one of the most difficult and heart-wrenching issues of our lives. Somewhere around September 1968, my maternal great-grandmother died. She had lived a full life and, as far as I know, simply died of old age. While any death is tragic, there was nothing particularly disturbing about the way she died. However, at the family dinner following the funeral, without warning, my mother became mentally deranged and began shoving dishes of food off the table. Efforts to calm her were futile. She acted so severely that she had to be put in a psychiatric hospital for several months. No one has ever been able to explain why she snapped like she did. The doctors diagnosed her as being bipolar, more commonly known today as manic-depressive, an emotional disorder characterized by dramatic and sometimes violent mood swings, although Mom was never violent to us. By this time, Steve was 12, I was 11 and Tom was 7. We were too young for Dad to leave us alone when he went to work. He had no choice but to send us to live with our grandparents. Dad sent Steve to our maternal grandparents, and Tom and I to live with Dad's mother and stepfather. Since they did not live in our school district, Tom and I had to abruptly change schools during the school year.

My paternal grandfather had died when I was only five years old. Three years later, my grandmother, Henrietta, remarried. His name was Peter DeHaan, a first-generation Dutch immigrant who spoke English with a heavy accent. He was a quiet man, which was not a problem since Grandma talked enough for both of them. He loved us as if we were his own and we reciprocated and came to think of him as our "real" grandpa.

Grandpa had two grown children with his first wife, who had also died. By the time Tom and I came to live with them, they had both been "empty nesters" for some time. Grandma kept a neat, clean house and I am sure it must have been a trial for them to have us there, but they never complained. Since both sets of grandparents lived right in Grand Rapids, Dad was able to take us home on the weekend, so they got a bit of a break and we got to be together as a family and go to our own church—minus Mom.

By this time, school had already started and changing schools for the second time in three months was hard on me. I was in the sixth grade and school had already started. Changing schools was hard on me. Although my teacher treated me with great kindness and compassion, my classmates, quite naturally, had already formed their own circle of friends and picked their own teams for ballgames during recess, so I was alone in a crowd. Except for two children of my dad's cousins who attended the same school, I do not recall making a single friend during this time. Thankfully, going to our own church on the weekends kept me connected with my friends there. But in looking back, I am sure that my greatest pain during that time came from our being separated as a family.

There were, however, some lighter moments. Grandma knew that I was a diehard Tigers' fan, and she would allow me to listen to the games on the radio in bed at night, as long as I was quiet. I often fell asleep with the game still on. That year, the Tigers won first place in the American League and went on to play in the World Series. On the night that they captured first place; sleep was the furthest thing from my mind. My bedroom was on the second floor and when the Tigers won that game, I got out of bed, ran to the stairwell and hollered the good news down to my grandparents below. To my utter amazement, my grandmother simply said something like, "Oh, that's nice," and showed no excitement whatsoever! To my 11-year-old mind, apart from God and family, nothing was more important than baseball—certainly not school!!

In that day, all World Series games were played during the daytime. My challenge was that I was in school when the games were on, but I was not to be denied. I do not remember if my grandmother ever knew what I did (probably not), but I carried a small transistor radio to school in my pocket and threaded an earpiece up my back on the inside of my shirt and listened to the games while in class, hoping that my teacher would be struck with temporary blindness. If she ever noticed, she never said anything. If I recall correctly, I was not the only boy doing so. To my great joy, the Tigers won the series in spectacular fashion.

My parents never approved of gambling as a rule, but my grandmother did not mind a bit of it. Every Monday night, my dad came over for dinner and stayed afterward to play penny poker with my grandparents and other relatives or friends. No serious money was ever in play. I think the main purpose was just an evening of entertainment with family and friends. Since my dad never did this at any other time, I think the main reason he did this was to be near us and not have to go home to an empty house. I am sure this must have been a lonely time for him.

In early January, 1969, after being in the hospital about four months, Mom was able to come home and so did we. We went back to our regular school and life became normal again, at least for a while. However, no one realized that the trauma that began during this time would leave deep emotional scars in me that would not fully surface for another forty years. What we could not have known is that the worst was still ahead of us. What we did not know was that this was just the beginning of a long, long road through Mom's emotional illness that would last until she passed away more than thirty years later. No one knows for sure, but I estimate that Mom had to be hospitalized at least fifty times for emotional and mental issues. At one point, she was on medication to the tune of twenty-one pills a day, although some of them were likely for other causes. When she was home, she was a kind, loving, attentive and godly wife and mother who created a lot of wonderful memories for us kids. But we could never predict when she would slide downhill emotionally and be hospitalized again, again, and again, leaving a hole in our lives that even my father, as heroically as he tried, could not completely fill.

My dad never blamed my mom for her problems and he was never ashamed of her, nor did she ever deny her problems. Our extended family never blamed my mother either, nor did friends and church members, to the best of my knowledge. All rallied to our support as best as they could. They will likely never know how desperately we needed them. Because mental illness carried a heavy negative stigma at the time, these attitudes were refreshing, and I believe provided us with at least some healthy coping mechanisms.

There was, however, one exception. One lady, who was not a close friend, remarked to another person in my hearing that Mom's problems were because of her children. When my dad found out about it, he made it clear that it was not true, but I carried the pain of that remark in my heart for years. I struggled to forgive that lady but eventually did so. It helps to remember that forgiveness is a choice, not a feeling. But I need to make one other comment. In situations where people are at a loss to know what to say, or are not well informed on the situation, silence would be the better part of valor. Thankfully, we did not have too many people like this in our lives. Ultimately, my dad's efforts to hold our family together, along with lots of help from family and friends, were successful, but the cost was high.

CHAPTER 2

Junior High and High School

In 1969, we moved to a larger home about six miles north of where we had lived. This meant changing schools again but not churches. This change was also hard for me. By this time, I was in the seventh grade. It did not help that I got sick and missed the first two weeks of school. My mother had to literally pull me out from under my bed to get me to go to school the first day. At school things went from bad to worse. The kids immediately labelled me with a nickname that I hated, but which, unfortunately, stuck with me all through high school. The mocking let up after a while and my classmates gradually accepted me, but most never did call me by my real name. I learned that the adage that "sticks and stones may break my bones, but names will never hurt me," simply is not true. From that experience, I vowed to call a person by their name unless they said that they wanted me to be called by something else.

Despite the difficulties, I began to make some friends. One of them was Bill Rienks, who lived a few blocks north of us. Bill came from a broken home and was not a Christian, to the best of my recollection. In some respects, we did not have a lot in common, except that we both were social misfits at school, which was enough to bond us together as best friends throughout high school. We normally walked to school together and just enjoyed being in each other's company. It was with Bill, however, that I would get into my one and only brush with the law just before graduation.

That year I also made my initial foray into the working world. Steve got a paper route with the Grand Rapids Press, and Dad urged me to do the same. He did this because he wanted me to learn the value of work. However, this meant would have to quit playing on the seventh-grade basketball team, which I had just joined, since our practice time after school coincided with the time of day that I had to deliver the papers.

My dad, in the typical Reformed tradition, had a strong work ethic and went to work faithfully every day to provide for our needs. In these years, Dad was not too verbal in expressing his love for us, but my mom would tell us that he expressed his love by providing for us. For Dad, the sweat of a man's brow was a badge of honor. It was a man's duty to provide for his family and he did everything he could to teach us about work from our earliest age. Mom thought he should give us a bit more time to enjoy growing up, but he never backed away from his convictions, and as a result all three of us boys have been hard workers all our lives. In my case, I became a workaholic, which had some negative effects down the road, but that story will have to wait.

Dad and I made an agreement. I would quit basketball and get a paper route. In turn, he agreed to let me quit the paper route and play football when I entered the ninth grade. I knew Dad would keep his promise, and I went to work. My route covered about one half of our street and the next two streets to the west of us. The neighbors were friendly and I enjoyed the work. Since our house was on my route, Dad knew he would have no problem getting his paper. My duties also included collecting the subscription fees every week and meeting with our boss every Saturday. I had to pay a certain amount for each paper and whatever was leftover was my pay. Here, I learned a concrete lesson that there are positive rewards for hard work.

One of the most traumatic events in my life happened sometime around 1971, when I was in the eighth grade. My mom had been in and out of several mental institutions by this time and saw a psychiatrist regularly. When she was home, she would get us up every morning and send us off to school with a good breakfast and lots of love. One morning, however, I woke up at the normal time and did not hear any movement in the kitchen downstairs and wondered why Mom had not awakened us.

I went downstairs and entered their bedroom and found Mom still in bed. No matter how hard I tried, I could not wake her up, and her skin was cold and clammy. Although I could tell she was alive because I saw her breathing, there are no words to describe the terror that gripped my young heart. I knew what I had to do. Dad had posted his work telephone number inside one of the kitchen cabinets near the telephone, and repeatedly told us that we could call him at work if we really needed him. I wasted no time in doing so.

Dad and I have discussed what happened next many times over the years and have yet to figure out how he got home so fast. We have also never figured out why neither of us thought to call an ambulance. Dad simply picked Mom up and carried her out the door and took her to the hospital himself. As he was doing so, I remember asking "Dad, what do you want us to do?" He replied kindly, "Go to school." In retrospect, there was not much else we could have done. I am sure it was best that we did not go with him to the hospital. I have no memory of when my two brothers got involved in the situation since we were all home at the time, but I seriously doubt that we learned anything in school that day, nor did Dad necessarily expect that of us.

Fortunately, the doctors and nurses at the hospital were able to revive Mom. They determined that she had intentionally overdosed on her depression medication and concluded that she had attempted suicide. This would be the first of at least four attempts to take her own life. The trauma of that day also would not fully surface in my life for nearly forty years. Even now, although I have worked through a lot of the pain, my emotions are still somewhat raw in recalling that horrible day.

Mom spent the next ten months in a state mental hospital in Kalamazoo, Michigan, about fifty miles south of where we lived. We were allowed to visit on Sunday afternoons and we faithfully did so. At first

Mom was required to stay inside so we visited in her room. We also saw rooms with straps on the beds where they would restrain patients that were potentially violent to themselves or others. Mom was one of those, although I thankfully do not recall ever actually seeing her strapped down. Sometimes, she was so heavily medicated that she was in something like a zombie state. She knew we were there and knew who we were, but it was hard to carry on a conversation with her. We still were on our best behavior so as not to upset her, which was a real challenge for two teenagers and Tom, who was only 11 at the time.

But there is a silver lining in this cloud. We made the weekly trip to Kalamazoo as fun as we could. Dad would make a picnic lunch to eat along the way. We would head out after church Sunday morning and stop to have lunch. Dad would either make Kool-Aid or we would stop and buy soft drinks. We would normally arrive at the hospital in time for the beginning of visiting hours at 2 p.m. and stay until the end at 4 p.m. No matter how good or poorly Mom was doing on the day we visited, we stayed until we had to leave. The evening service at church started at 5 p.m., which we normally attended faithfully. During this time, however, it was too much for Dad to do all in one day, so we usually just went home.

Today, we look back at that time and recognize that those Sunday trips and picnics on the way to the hospital were a real bonding time between Dad and us boys. That bond, though strained at times, has remained strong all our lives. Not long ago, I asked Dad how he survived all those years with everything that happened and he honestly said, "I don't know." My response is much the same, except to say that I think that bonding together as a family, with lots of support from family and friends, went a long way toward making a bad situation just a little bit better. The fact that my parents never denied my mom's problems, or tried to hide them, also surely helped.

By now, we were old enough to be at home by ourselves when Dad was not around. But this meant that we had to do more of the housework, and Dad had to continually get after us to do it. Being typical young males, we procrastinated as much as possible. In time, the hospital allowed Mom to come home on the weekends. Dad would go get her after work on Friday and take her back on Sunday afternoon, or after church Sunday night. Whenever Friday rolled around, Dad would say something like, "Now boys, don't clean the house too well or Mom might think we don't need her." Right. There was no chance that we would clean it too well under any circumstances!

After ten months, Mom improved and was the doctors finally released her from the hospital. But the cycle continued as she was in and out the hospital for emotional problems time and again until she died. As I grew up, I began to recognize that marriages all around us were falling apart and more and more men were walking out on their wives and families. One day, I asked my dad why he stayed with my mom all those years. Without even taking time to think about it, he looked me straight in the eye and simply said, "Dave, I made a promise to your mom on our wedding day." "For richer, for poorer, in sickness and in health, 'til death do us part." Dad's unconditional commitment to keeping his promises kept our family together.

My dad is my hero.

As I have thought about this through the years, I had to confront some questions, some of which were faith-challenging. I have done my best to face these issues squarely. What made Mom like this? Quite honestly, I have never known the answer to this question. But there is at least one strong clue of what may have contributed to it. Mom never had a good relationship with her father. In many ways, her father was a good man who looked after the needs of his family, and I believe that he was a Christian. He attended church faithfully all his life, although I do not recall him talking about faith much, and Grandma always said grace at the table when we were with them. But he was also an austere and emotionally distant man. Like others in his generation, he had come of age and married in the early years of the American Great Depression, which may have contributed to his austerity. Beyond that, however, the roots of the issues will always be a mystery.

To their credit and, most probably, mostly because of Grandma, Mom and Grandpa did maintain a cordial relationship, lived in the same town much of my parent's married life, and saw each other regularly. Mom had a great relationship with her mother, and was reasonably close to her siblings, who all lived within an hour's drive of each other nearly all their lives. She made a great effort to get along with her dad, and to be fair, I think he did the same. Yet the underlying issues were never resolved, to the best of my knowledge.

But there was another question that I had to confront, and this one impacted me more seriously. This was the question, "How could a woman who obviously loved God, her husband and her children, even think of trying to kill herself?" I do not recall that Mom ever answered the question, nor did anyone else. I do seem to recall that I asked her once if she had thought through what the impact of her suicide would be on her family, and I believe she answered that she had not. A key element in depression is that the depressed person can become so self-absorbed that they are not aware of how their actions impact those who love them.

Like the other issues, I had to leave this question of why someone would even think of this with God. In the final analysis, that was the best thing I could have done, as God alone knows all the answers. Decades later, when I had my own battle with deep depression, I gained some insights that may have at least partially answered the question.

Since I knew that Mom did not want to be depressed, I never blamed her for what she experienced. Much later, however, I had to come to grips with the fact that Mom was morally responsible for how she dealt with it, specifically when it came to attempting suicide, an action that one could hardly construe as accidental. Then I needed to confront the issue of forgiveness, but now I am getting ahead of my story.

Like any other situation in life, there was a brighter side. Mom made numerous friends with other women during her various hospitalizations who were also dealing with depression or other emotional issues, and they remained friends after she got out. She would spend hours on the phone with them, and regularly visited back and forth with those living in the Grand Rapids area, providing loving support for one another. While she later grew apart from some of them, some remained friends for the rest of her life, and were a great blessing to her, and she to them.

During Mom's various hospitalizations, those who sent a card, or showed in some other way that they cared, touched her deeply. When she got out of the hospital, she began sending cards to others in need, or for any other occasion, happy or sad. I would estimate that she averaged several cards a week for at least twenty-five years, endearing her to those within her circle of influence. Cards were expensive even back in the 70s, but I do not recall that my dad ever complained. Not only did she bless others in this manner, but I think it also helped her make sense of her own pain. I later learned that suffering is easier to bear if you can see a purpose in it, and I think Mom did.

My parents always took notice when people they knew were suffering. For example, when their church started a prayer chain to pray for those in need, they joined.[1] When someone they knew was sick, they prayed, and brought meals. They visited those in the hospital. When even the most casual acquaintance died, or lost someone close to them, they always visited the family or attended the funeral if possible. After Dad retired and had more time, they often did both.

Meanwhile, life went on. True to his word, Dad allowed me to quit my paper route when I entered the ninth grade so that I could play football. I had never played, but I knew the game well from watching games on TV. That year, we won as many games as we lost, so we came out even. I was not in the starting lineup in many games, if any at all, but I played well enough the same guys that, two years before, had mocked

---

[1] A prayer chain is when someone calls the pastor or head of the prayer chain with a request. That person would then telephone the next person on the list, who would call the next person, etc., until they got to the end of the list. Then, everyone on the prayer chain would pray about the request.

me and given me the unwanted nickname, voted me the team's most improved player. I was touched by the honor. I went on to play the entire four years of high school. Our teams were not all that good, but we enjoyed playing anyway.

I also played basketball for three years in school. By the time I finished high school I was 6'4" tall. I had grown tall fast, but my muscle coordination developed at a more normal pace, meaning that I was rather uncoordinated, and like football, I spent most of the time on the bench. My interest in playing baseball had waned, probably in part because the house in which we now lived was not as conducive to practicing in the back yard as the other house had been. I got less playing time because my skills had not continued to develop, and I stopped playing after my freshman year.[2] Apparently, I was not destined to become a professional athlete.

I was an average student with a teenager's view of the world, meaning that it did not extend beyond high school. As long as my grades were good enough to allow me to play sports, I was happy. My love of reading did not result in a passion for homework! The seeds that would later result in a great love of research, learning and critical reflection had yet to germinate, even though I did make the dean's list one semester.

When I was 15, Dad, with his solid work ethic, began to push Steve, who was 16, to get a part-time job. Steve, whose view of the future was probably not larger than mine, was in no hurry to do so. He enjoyed coming home after school and listening to music on his record player— an ancestor of today's CDs. I heard from a friend about job openings at a local Big Boys, a national restaurant chain, and was determined to get a job before Dad started pushing me as well, so I planned to go with my friend to apply without telling Steve. When I told Dad what I was going to do, he insisted that Steve go with us to apply. Despite my selfish motive, we all got jobs as busboys, cleaning tables after customers had

---

[2]In America, the high school years are labelled freshman, sophomore, junior and senior.

left, and helping the waitresses with whatever else they needed. We usually put in two ten-hour shifts on Friday and Saturday nights, working well into the early hours of the next morning, which made staying awake in church rather difficult. I later became a "jack-of-all-trades" and mastered the dishwasher and cash register, along with cooking on occasion, and even serving as a waiter one night when we were short of waitresses.

I worked at Big Boys for about two years, but Steve and our friend worked there much longer. Two things happened to Steve during this time that radically changed his life. First, he eventually met a young waitress named Terrie and fell madly in love. They went on to have 31 happy years of marriage and three wonderful children before she succumbed to cancer at the age of 55. Second, Steve, who was not whole-heartedly serving the Lord at the time, got acquainted with a church group that frequented the restaurant after their Sunday night service and, through them, he and Terrie got radically saved. The power of God transformed their lives. Their church was Pentecostal, and Steve became the first one in our family to be baptized in the Holy Spirit, which initially got a mixed reaction from our staunchly Christian Reformed family! He has been faithful in his walk with God ever since.

In September, 1973, I entered the school's job co-op program, meaning that I only went to school in the morning and got credit for working a job in the afternoons. Through this program, I got another job at another restaurant called the Swiss Chalet, washing dishes and cooking. For a while, between the two jobs I worked about forty hours a week, but I did not mind. I was tired of school anyway. Since I worked at the Swiss Chalet in lieu of going to school, I still had time for sports.

About a year later, I got a job in a local mall at Turn-Style, a small Michigan-based department store chain and quit the restaurant jobs. As luck would have it, they sent me to work in the toy department! Given my penchant for fun, it was a perfect fit for me. The job also paid better than the restaurants did. This gave me the opportunity to learn a little about the retail sales industry. The core philosophy was to take care of the customer, doing your best to help them get what they wanted, and being nice even if they were not. Working here during the Christmas season could best be described as a period of shoppers' insanity. Our aisles were stacked so high with merchandise, even a tall guy like me could not see over the top. From about 6 p.m. until closing at 10 p.m., people mobbed the aisles, many of whom asked for help to find what they wanted. We would occasionally need to seek respite from the crowds by going into the storeroom in the back to get more merchandise to put on the shelves. It was fun but tiring. I think I stayed on there until I finished high school.

Socially, I felt awkward about girls, so I usually admired the pretty ones from afar and did not date much, despite my parents' repeated invitation to bring a girl home for dinner. Late in my senior year, one of my mom's friends wanted to set me up with a young lady, so I agreed. It was the one and only time that I ever dated a non-Christian and I had the opportunity to lead her to the Lord several months later. Nevertheless, I do not condone "missionary dating" under any circumstances. The result is usually heartache and I Corinthians 6 clearly forbids it. The relationship eventually died of natural causes as we gradually went our separate ways in the year or so after we graduated high school.

I also did a bit of traveling in high school. We normally took our family vacations in Michigan, but once (which I think was the year that Mom was hospitalized for nearly a year), Dad took us boys on a trip to Wisconsin to see the Wisconsin Dells, a river with some beautifully colored rock formations. Since Mom was in the hospital, she could not go, but we had a great time, and visited Mom on the way back to tell her all about it.

One Christmas we all packed up and drove to Florida to celebrate the holidays with Grandpa and Grandma DeHaan, the ones with whom Tom and I had lived when Mom was first hospitalized for depression.

Like many retirees from Michigan, they lived in Florida in the winter after Grandpa retired to avoid Michigan's harsh winter weather.

During Spring Break in my senior year of high school, Steve and a friend, Rick, and I packed up Steve's car and took off for Massachusetts to see an old girlfriend of Rick's. We also wanted to see the historical sites around Boston—the birthplace of the American Revolution back in the 18th century. Mom was worried that we would get lost, but Dad reminded Mom that he had taught us how to read a map and he was confident that we would be fine. Except for one situation where we misread the map and went about 180 miles out of the way, we did just fine and had a great week out on our own.

A few weeks later, the entire senior class took a bus trip to New York. We were only gone about three days and we had a great time seeing the sites, which included the Empire State Building, the United Nations and the Statue of Liberty. We also took in the two World Trade Center buildings, which were still standing at the time. I remember that we spent one night in a hotel. Several of my classmates chose to drink and party the night away, but a friend and I decided we were going to get a good night's sleep, and get up early to go sightseeing on our own before rejoining our classmates later in the day. Neither of us had ever been to New York before, and we had no way of knowing if we would ever return, so we made the most of it, and I was glad we did. I came back tired but happy.

As I have already mentioned, God, church and family were the center of our lives. We saw our grandparents regularly. Mom had a brother who was about ten years younger than she was, and a sister that was seventeen years younger. Because of their age differences, she never developed much of a relationship with her sister until later in life, but she always had a good relationship with her brother. Dad had one sister who was two years younger than him. We did not see Mom's brother and his family, nor Dad's sister and her family, too often because they lived outside of Grand Rapids, but they were all part of our lives.

Not only did we faithfully attend church every Sunday, we also participated in weeknight activities. Our denomination had a boys' group called the Calvinist Cadet Corps that we were all involved in and we later moved up to the youth group when we became teenagers. We also attended Sunday school and Daily Vacation Bible School during the summer. Being a part of these activities was as natural as breathing to us.

I cannot say with any certainty when I came to know Christ. I remember telling my mom when I was about eight that I wanted to serve the Lord. Attending evangelistic rallies was not really a part of our church tradition, but we did attend one night when an evangelist came and held a citywide rally, and I responded to the altar call. I forgot all about the experience until I was rereading an old journal in researching this book, so apparently the experience did not make a permanent impression on me.

Like any teenager, I was susceptible to peer pressure. Since Dad occasionally had a beer, I saw no harm in going to football beer parties on occasion and drinking a bit, although I never became drunk—and my parents saw no harm in it. I also began to use some inappropriate language behind my mother's back, and I also went to movies of which they would not approve. I was not rejecting my faith, but I was testing it to know for myself if it was true. Fortunately, God had me on a short leash, and my period of semi-rebellion did not last long.

Our church baptized infants and we were all duly baptized within a couple months of our births. Our church also had a tradition of requiring those that wished to join the church as adults to make what we called a "profession of faith." This resulted in me meeting with the church leaders during their monthly meetings and answering questions about my personal faith in Christ. Like others my age, I chose to do this during my senior year in high school, shortly before my 18th birthday. Then they invited me to make a confession of faith before the entire church during a Sunday morning worship service. This involved answering "yes" or "no" to a few simple questions, which the pastor asked from the pulpit, and I answered while standing at my pew. The questions were not hard, but they were meaningful, and did require a serious response.

This was a big deal for my family. At least one set of grandparents attended, and perhaps others as well, although the passage of time has dimmed my memory a bit. The service went well and my mother went out of her way to put on a big Sunday dinner for all members of the family as a celebration of the event. Many reaffirmed me for what I had done, and that encouraged me. I took the event seriously but with joy.

Around this time, I also heard about a summer missions' program sponsored by our denomination, called Summer Workshop in Ministries (SWIM). I became interested in serving for a summer, although I had no clue at the time that I would be going into full-time ministry. I think one had to be a full member of a church to qualify, which may have been what spurred me to make my confession of faith when I did.

By this time, I was in my last year of high school, and was not really sure what I wanted to do with my life. At this point, I did not know how to seek God's guidance regarding such a decision. I got a course catalog from a local college and decided that political science looked like an interesting major to pursue. Then, I had to face the decision of how I could afford college if I spent the summer with SWIM. While waiting to meet with the elders of the church when I went to make my profession of faith, I laid the matter out before the Lord. In prayer, I committed to going on the summer missions' trip and leaving the matter of funding college in the hands of the Lord. That decision ultimately led me down a path I had not anticipated, and resulted in some of the greatest adventures of my life. I never did study political science.

Not long afterwards, I received a phone call from a recruiter for the United States Navy, a practice that was common among all branches of the U.S. military. They would call all young men who were about to graduate from high school. I told the man I was not interested and that I was going to college. Then, he started talking about how the Navy would pay my way to college if I served a four-year hitch in the Navy first. That got my attention! I told him I would think it over and let him know. The more I thought about it, the more I liked it. My dad had served in the Army in the Korean War in the 1950s, and my parents supported the idea of me serving in the military. Right after my 18th birthday, the day I legally became an adult, I signed the paperwork to enter the Navy six months from then, in October 1975, leaving my summer free to participate in the SWIM program. But first, I had a brush with the law.

As graduation day in June grew near, the weather started getting hot. On one unusually hot day in May, Bill Rienks came by and invited me to go swimming with him in a nearby city park that had a small manmade lake, which served as a swimming hole for the community. When I reminded him that the park was not yet open for the swimming season, and that to go swimming might get us in trouble, he explained that he had found a way to get through the fence that surrounded it, and he was sure that there would not be any problem. Teenagers are not known for their wisdom and I went along. We had a great time—until the police caught us coming back through the fence on our way home. The police took us to the police station in a squad car, where they fingerprinted and booked us. Then, they took us next door to the local courthouse and hauled us in front of a judge while we were still in our wet swimming gear, and our hair—which extended to the bottom of our ears at the time—was still matted from swimming. Our appearance doomed us, and we quickly pleaded guilty to "disturbing the peace," which was a misdemeanor and not a serious crime. The judge gave us a choice of paying a fine or spending three weeks in jail—which would have interfered with my summer ministry plans! In a rare flash of intelligent thinking, we decided to pay the fines.

Years later, when I went to Japan for ministry, the immigration form I had to fill out asked if I had ever been convicted of a crime. I answered honestly to the immigrant agent, who did not speak English well. I thought he was going to deny me entry. After several frustrating moments of trying to explain myself, exasperated, he finally stamped a visa into my passport and, thankfully, let me into the country.

Shortly after high school graduation, a small team of six young people, four ladies and two men, including me, boarded a plane in Grand Rapids and flew to Utah, for our six-week SWIM team missions' experience. We landed in Salt Lake City, where we were picked up and driven about forty miles north to Ogden, where the church we would be serving was located. Ogden was in the Rocky Mountains and the nearby mountains were called the Wasatch range. The tallest mountain there was Ben Lomond with its summit at nearly 10,000 feet above sea level. Ogden lay at the foot of that mountain.

We lived with people in the church. They assigned Steve (the other young man in the group) and me to stay with a young couple, Paul and Linda Smith, who were expecting their first baby. They were a pleasant couple and we got on well, both with them and with each other. A young man in the church named Bill joined our team, making a total of seven members. I do not recall all our activities, but some of them remain vivid in my mind. One, I preached my first sermon in a local street mission for drunks and homeless people. It is probably just as well that my notes from that first message no longer survive. We also conducted a Vacation Bible School and I think we did follow up from house to house with the parents who sent their kids. They trained us in D. James Kennedy's *Evangelism Explosion* program, which focused on training people for personal evangelism in home visitation. We did lead at least one lady to the Lord and we were all excited about that. It was a great experience.

The greatest lesson I learned during that time was that serving the Lord could be a lot of fun. I had no clue at this point that within one year, God would call me into the ministry. When he did so, this experience gave me confidence that serving the Lord in ministry could be a wonderful experience.

Later that summer, I attended a young people's church convention in Bellingham, Washington. It was my first trip to the west coast. At the end of the convention, we spent the day in Seattle before flying home. Little did I know then that the woman I would later marry was attending a college in Seattle at that time.

On October 9, 1975, my dad took me to the bus station to travel to Detroit where I was inducted into active duty status in the U.S. Navy. Life as I had known it would never be the same.

CHAPTER 3

Sailing the Seas and Some Unexpected Encounters with God

I was the first child to permanently leave home. The Navy had an entrance and examination station in Detroit where I was sworn in and given medical tests. Then, they took me to the airport to fly to Orlando, Florida, to undergo basic training, better known as "boot camp." Once in Orlando, I was assigned to a training company with seventy-nine other guys and sent to the company barracks, a long room with about eighty beds—all stacked in bunk bed style.

The next morning, all eighty of us were awakened at 5 a.m. and marched to the base barber shop to get our first military haircut. Standing in line that morning, I recognized that I could not hide my faith from my "roommates," since we were going to be together 24/7 for the next nine weeks. I realized that I had a choice to make. I could either walk away from what I believed, or I could embrace it with all my heart, soul, mind and strength. There would be no middle ground for me. I chose to embrace Jesus, which meant, among other things, reading my Bible and praying in sight of my peers, since the only place we had any privacy was the toilet. Since then, I have never looked back, nor have I ever been ashamed of my decision. I found some other Christians in my company, including one man who was an ordained lay Baptist minister. We became a band of brothers for the duration of boot camp. One new friend, a guy named Dave Humphreys, became a good friend and would share some adventures with me beyond our time in Orlando.

The next stop was the supply department where we were herded like cattle to get our uniforms and other military gear. We were finally beginning to look like sailors, although acting like one would take a little longer. We were also introduced to military food, which we called "chow." Since the mess hall (cafeteria) had to serve a couple of thousand people three meals a day, it would be fair to say that the cooking was somewhat different than Mom's cooking at home!

From day one, the Navy's aim was to prepare us for Navy life. Military discipline and protocol were strictly enforced. We marched as a group everywhere we went, and we learned how to salute our superiors. We did security watches at night and stood for inspections regularly during the day. We did marching drills out on the parade grounds again, again and again. We also underwent physical training, which included obstacle courses. We were taught how to fold our clothes and make our beds military-style. The point was not so much about cleanliness as it was to determine if we knew how to follow orders, which could save our lives, or the lives of our shipmates, in a combat situation. The Navy had zero tolerance for insubordination and lack of discipline. In boot camp, they were only interested in our obedience, not our opinions—even though we had plenty of them!

The Navy did care about our spiritual needs and had chaplains stationed on base to conduct chapel services on Sunday morning and provide other services as needed. There were two types of services for Protestants to attend. One was contemporary and the other more conservative. If I recall correctly, the differences were mainly in music styles. Raised as I was in the staider style of the Christian Reformed Church, I opted for the conservative service and the old hymns.

My mother wrote faithfully every week and I often wrote back. We were occasionally allowed to call home. My parents were always glad to hear from me and it helped keep the family bonds tight and my homesickness at bay. They were proud to have a son serving his country. They were also glad to know that my Christian faith remained strong in a non-Christian environment.

Finally, after nine weeks of drills, classes, inspections, physical testing and a million-and-one other things, it was time to graduate and move on. Some graduates had family members who came, but mine did not. The plan for graduation day was to march around the parade grounds in formation in our dress uniforms. And then, we would stand at parade rest[1] before the reviewing stand while speeches were made.

---

[1]Parade rest is a military standing position with legs spread apart and hands clasped behind one's back.

Since the weather was extremely hot and our dress uniforms for that time of year meant wearing a military coat and tie, there was some concern that we might faint while standing still for a long period of time. We were warned about this and told to be sure to flex our legs while standing in formation and not allow our knees to lock. Hospital corpsmen with stretchers were on standby, suggesting that trouble was afoot.

Sure enough, while some admiral was droning on about how wonderful the Navy was, and how we were performing our patriotic duty in serving our country and its noble citizens, I was one of those who fainted. Because I was tall, I almost knocked over one or two of the men behind me in formation. A couple of corpsmen rushed out, rolled me over onto a stretcher and ingloriously carried me off the field in front of the gawking crowd. They took me to the other side of the field, where they had water and other such things to revive me. My only injury was a bruised ego, which when I recovered, was partially assuaged by rejoining my company for the final victorious march around the parade grounds. Then, it was time to head for the airport for a two-week furlough in Grand Rapids over the Christmas holidays.

After two wonderful weeks at home, where my proud parents insisted that I wear my dress uniform to church, I set off for my next duty station, the Naval Training Center in San Diego, California. I flew there and had a connecting flight in Chicago's O'Hare International Airport, the busiest airport in the world at the time. Much to my surprise, my boot camp buddy, Dave Humphreys, was on the same flight! Only God could have arranged this. That Dave was going to San Diego on the same day was not coincidental, because it was a popular training base, and we had both left boot camp on the same day with the same amount of allotted leave. Since he was from Ohio, I should not have been surprised that he was connecting through Chicago like I was, but to be on the same flight out of the busiest airport in the world was nothing short of amazing to me.

We landed in San Diego about 10 p.m. on a Friday night and made our way to the base. It was a strange feeling, as it was the first time I had been away from home with no one supervising me. On both the summer missions' trips to Ogden, and the weeks in basic training, someone else scheduled my life and told me where to go and when to go there. Now, as long as I showed up for training, the Navy really did not care what I did—as long as it was legal. Soon after arriving, I found out that San Diego had more brothels than any other city in America. But I had made a choice to follow Jesus and had no trouble avoiding such fleshpots, although many sailors felt free to indulge. But being away from home, I began to feel a void in my life that God would fill in a most wonderful way.

My friend, Dave, was also a committed Christian who happened to be Presbyterian. He and I decided that the first thing in the morning, we would go out and look for either a Presbyterian or Christian Reformed Church to attend the following Sunday. Apparently, it never dawned on us to consider attending the base chapel. In a day before Google made such searches easy, we had to locate a church simply by going off base and walking the streets. We could have used a telephone directory, but neither of us had been to the city before, and had no idea what streets were near the base. Since it was a Saturday, and no one would be answering the telephone at any church we might have called, walking around until we found a church was the only real option. Fortunately, we found a Presbyterian church just a few blocks from the base; we happily presented ourselves at Sunday School and church the following morning.

My contract with the Navy guaranteed me a chance to train to become a radioman. At that time, the use of Morse Code was being phased out and our training focused on radio teletype, an ancestor to today's email, and voice communications. We were trained to communicate both with other ships and with shore stations. The training was more tedious than difficult: learning to read ticker tapes that came out of the teletype machines, tuning transmitters and receivers, and a hundred-and-one other things that we needed to know once we were assigned to a ship.

In my room in the barracks, I had no choice regarding who my three roommates would be. The ones I got were absolute pagans and, to their credit, made no claim to be anything else. They partied, slept around, and generally carried on the life of an average sailor. I am not sure they knew what to make of me. I had a Bible and several Christian books in my possession that I made no effort to hide. I went to church or Bible study several times a week, unless my Navy duties took priority. They made fun of me and I am sure I did not always bear it with grace. After a couple of months, I convinced two of them to go to church with me.

They, in turn, dragged the other one out of bed and made him go with us. It was a powerful service that day. While they did not come to Christ, the mocking stopped.

Dave and I met regularly at meal time. He was in training for another job classification, so I usually only saw him at meals, church or Bible study. As we met other Christians on base, we invited them to join us for meals and fellowship, and ended up with a respectable number. We just found a good place in the mess hall, pulled some chairs and tables together and enjoyed being together. Different church affiliations made no difference to us. We welcomed all who claimed to follow the Savior.

Navy women were called Waves, and there were plenty of them on base and in our classes. Aside from not being allowed to enter their barracks, there were no prohibitions on fraternization like there had been in boot camp. One day, Dave introduced a young female sailor named Kathy to the lunch group, and she became a regular member. She was attending an Assemblies of God church. She had found someone with a van who offered to bring her to church and told her to invite all her friends.

I gladly accepted the invitation, but I must confess that I was more interested in Kathy than I was the Assemblies of God. Piling in the van along with others one day, I had no idea that this would become one of the greatest turning points in my life. From the beginning, the church members wrapped their arms around me as if I was one of their own. Being a young guy who was out on his own for the first time, I was drawn to their love and acceptance like a bear drawn to honey. I was drawn back to the church because of the way they received me. I found out later that Kathy had a boyfriend back home, so she never returned my interest, and I let it go, but she did become a faithful friend. After a few weeks, however, Dave returned to the Presbyterian church.

The only problem I had with the Assemblies of God was that they were Pentecostal and I was not, nor did I wish to be at the time. The reason I was not initially interested in becoming Pentecostal had more to do with personal prejudice than anything else, and I had made some comments about Pentecostals that I would later regret. My attitude probably came from the fact that the CRC did not believe in the Baptism in the Holy Spirit with speaking in other tongues, so I had no experience with this as a child. Since I assumed uncritically that the CRC was correct,

I was automatically skeptical about anything the CRC did not practice or endorse.

My older brother, Steve, had no such inhibitions and was attending a Oneness, independent, Pentecostal church. I accepted Steve's invitation to attend a Sunday night service with him and Terrie before joining the Navy, and was less than thrilled with what I saw. To put it mildly, the praise and worship part of the service was much more casual, informal and spontaneous than I had ever seen. There were lots of arms in the air, shouting, dancing and all manner of such things that were most certainly not done in the CRC! We were two hours into the service before the preacher even got to the pulpit! The CRC services never lasted more than an hour and fifteen minutes. I was appalled!

On the other hand, I had to admit that Jesus had radically changed Steve, who by this time had come to know Christ and had been baptized in the Holy Spirit. The change in his attitude and lifestyle was evident to the whole family. So, I had to admit that Pentecostalism had been good for him, despite my reservations.

Now, however, I was in an interesting situation. I still had major reservations about Pentecostalism, but I really liked the people at the church, so I kept going. In what could only be described as the plan of God, it seemed like all the pastor's sermons and Wednesday night Bible studies were about the Holy Spirit! If I did not want to hear about it, it would have meant leaving the church and not being around such loving people. I was caught between a rock and a hard place! Slowly, lovingly, and tenderly the Lord broke down my defenses, and I began to hunger for the power of God in a way that I had never experienced.

Then it happened. One Wednesday night, following a Bible study, an older layman who had often been used in giving prophetic utterances and tongues and interpretation, came up to me and invited me to go with him down to the prayer room in the basement of the church. He explained that there were two young sailors like me, who wanted to rededicate their lives to the Lord, and he wanted me to come and support them. I was happy to do so. After leading these men in a prayer of rededication, he moved right into leading them into the Baptism in the Holy Spirit, and they began speaking in tongues and worshiping God.

Then I came forward and told the man that I did not need to rededicate my life to the Lord, but I also wanted to receive the Holy Spirit

Baptism. He responded by simply laying his hand on my chest and encouraged me to stop speaking in English. The Holy Spirit came upon me in that moment and words began coming out of my mouth that from that day until this I have never understood. This initial experience did not last long, but it was a watershed moment in my life. The Holy Spirit lit a fire in me that night that has never been extinguished.

There was an immediate change in my life. My passion for a deeper understanding of the Word of God dramatically increased. The Bible seemed to become a new book. My desire to see people come to know the Lord became consuming. Sometime afterwards, the Lord spoke to me that I needed to support missionaries in addition to tithing. This was also new to me. Giving to missions would be part of the beginning of one of the greatest adventures of my life.

Around the same time, I was walking on the base, probably going home from a midweek Bible study at the chapel, when God quietly said to my heart, "David, I want you to preach my gospel." There were no thunderclaps, revelations of Heaven, Hell or anything else. Rather, there was just a quiet assurance of his voice and presence. I quietly responded, "Yes, Lord," even though I had no clue as to what that would mean, where it would take me, or what it would cost me.

When God called me into the ministry, I assumed that he would find a way for me to leave the Navy. After all, how could I be in full-time ministry and still be in the Navy without going to school for several years to become a chaplain? I had a lot to learn. God's learning curve for me was rather long.

Going to Sea

Not long after this, I completed my training in radio communications and was sent to a small Navy salvage ship, the USS *Tawakoni*, affectionately dubbed the "Big T," which was homeported in Pearl Harbor, Hawaii. Because the movement of Navy ships was classified information, those who wrote my orders and arranged my travel were apparently not aware that the ship was in Japan when I arrived at the airport in Honolulu. Our ship was assigned to Service Squadron Five, which was a small collection of ships of our kind that were all based at Pearl Harbor. Two men from the Squadron's head office met me at the airport. They informed me of the situation, and said that I would stay on the base overnight while a decision was made whether to keep me on the base until my ship returned about six weeks later, or fly me to Japan.

Since I had the evening free and someone had given me the address to the First Assembly of God church in Honolulu, I headed into town to see a bit of the city and try to locate the church. I succeeded and actually found the senior pastor in the office doing counseling, and he had a free half-hour between appointments to visit with me. The relationship with the church that began that night continues to this day, although I have not been back to Hawaii for many years.

The following day, the Squadron leaders sent me to nearby Hickam Air Force Base and put me on a C-130 cargo plane bound for a U.S. Air Force base in Yokota, Japan. It was night when we arrived. The next day, I took a four-hour ride to the U.S. Navy base in Yokosuka, Japan, where my ship was in port.

Calling the *Tawakoni* the "Big T" was a misnomer. In reality, the entire ship was only 205 feet long and thirty-eight and a half feet across at its widest point.[2] Below the main deck, about fifty men were crammed into small birthing compartments. Sleeping bunks were stacked up in sets of three. About six officers shared small staterooms in the forward part of the ship. Only the captain and the executive officer had private quarters.

Arriving at night, sleep was the first priority. The next morning, I woke up and began to meet my shipmates. I was surprised to learn that our ship was too small to be assigned a chaplain, but I was delighted to find out that one Christian crewman was assigned to lead lay services on Sundays, when we were gone from our homeport. I quickly looked him up and we became friends.

I began to get acclimated to the ship and settle into my duties. Before long, I was just another member of the crew, although I was pretty naïve about the Navy, and life in general. I also did not immediately fit in well because of my Christian beliefs, which I had no intention of changing, despite their efforts to bring me with them to the bars. After I had been

---

[2]https://military.wikia.org/wiki/USS_Tawakoni_(ATF-114) (accessed April 27, 2020).

onboard a week or two, we set sail overnight across the Sea of Japan to Pusan (also spelled Busan), a bustling seaport on the southeastern coast of South Korea. We stayed about ten days before returning to Japan, and then setting sail for the two-week trip back to Pearl Harbor. By the time we arrived back at Pearl the ship had been gone over five months. The shipmates that were married were delighted to be reunited with their families.

With one exception, the trip home was uneventful. One Sunday while we were on the way back, I was invited to give the message at our Sunday service onboard, and I agreed. A few days before, a shipmate named Dennis LeBlanc asked if he could attend, even though all he had was a Gideon's New Testament. I told him that I was speaking from that part of the Bible anyway, and invited him. He did attend, and four days later I had the honor of leading him to Christ. The word of God took hold of him, and he began to share his new faith immediately. He became a member of the Navigators' group on base and would be my best friend until I left Pearl Harbor two years later. A few months later, the lay leader left our ship and I took his place. It was the first official ministry position I ever held.

When we returned to Hawaii, I reconnected to the First Assembly of God church, and began to get deeply involved. The winds of revival, known as the Charismatic Renewal, were blowing through Hawaii at that time and the church had hoisted their sails to catch the wind. We began hosting a special Monday night service known as "Pneuma Fellowship," and churches of all denominations, including Catholics and independents, were warmly welcomed. Special speakers from all different backgrounds, some of them quite well-known, came and ministered to us. I attended as often as my duties allowed, and I usually handled the sound booth up in a corner of the balcony of the church. This was my first real exposure to the broader Kingdom of God.

With two services on Sunday, Pneuma Fellowship on Monday nights, midweek services on Wednesday evenings, and the single's group on Friday nights, the church became the center of my life. Since my duties onboard the ship required that I remain onboard ship every fourth night to help guard the ship, as well as normal work hours during the day, I did not get to church every time the doors were open, but I could attend at least some of the meetings every week.

During this time, my love and understanding of missions began to bloom because our church had a heart for missions. Consistent with Matthew 6:21, I began to ask myself where the money I gave to missions was going, and God began to answer through the missionaries that visited our church. My heart was touched, and my interest soared when I heard about people coming to Christ all over the world, churches being planted, and Bible schools turning out leaders that would plant more churches, which would reach more people for Christ. This interest in missions would eventually result in God calling me to serve as a missionary, and that interest would become a lifelong passion.

My shipmates who were Christians and I began to meet every morning for prayer before the day's work began. Someone suggested that we write our prayer requests in a logbook and then record the occasions when God answered our prayers—or at least the times that he said, "Yes" to our requests. In time, we filled many pages with requests and answers. While the logbook is no longer in my possession, the memories of God's answers to our prayers have never been forgotten.

A little over a year after returning to Pearl Harbor, we set sail once again for the western Pacific, around June or July of 1977, to take our turn in patrolling the seas to keep them open for international trade. While we were at Pearl, I became friends with another sailor, Richard Yurkovic, who was also a part of our church. His ship, too, was bound for the western Pacific. Shortly before we left, we both agreed in prayer to ask the Lord to help us connect while we were in Asia. That prayer would be marvelously answered.

Our first stop was Guam, a small island American territory in the western Pacific that had a large Navy base. Our ship needed some repairs, and even though Pearl Harbor had excellent ship repair facilities, the powers that be, in their infinite wisdom, determined that our ship should be repaired in Guam. I do not recall if anyone ever explained the logic to us, nor were our opinions ever sought. The U.S. Navy was not a democracy!

From there we moved on to Subic Bay, Philippines, our unofficial home base over the next few months. From there we spent our share of time at sea, patrolling places like the South China Sea, where a lot of the world's trade passed through. We visited places like Hong Kong, Japan and Taiwan, as well as the Caroline Islands in the Pacific.

The time in the Philippines was the most memorable. The Subic Bay Naval Station was a large, fully equipped base that included a number of recreational places. The city outside the base, however, was filled with bars and brothels, which most of my shipmates frequented. I was far too adventurous to stay on base, but had no problem maintaining my testimony by staying away from places that would compromise my biblical morals. Like any human, I had my faults, but alcohol and loose women were not a major challenge. Yet it was only God's grace that I did not succumb to these temptations as well. If I recall correctly, my good friend Dennis opted to spend most of the time on base. He had grown significantly in the Lord and did not want to live the old sailor life. Our shipmates noticed the change in him.

When we arrived, I discovered that my friend Richard's ship was also in port. Having heard that there was a Christian serviceman's center in town, I looked for him and found him there and we had a joyous reunion. The serviceman's center was run by a missionary group called the Overseas Missionary Fellowship. Richard and I shared many happy hours there over the next few months. Since the center had a bunk room for guys wanting to get away from their ships, I often spent the weekends there when I had free time. On one occasion, Dennis and I took a bus to Baguio City, the summer capital of the Philippines, to attend a Christian retreat at a US Air Force base known as Camp John Hay. I had no idea that I would be living within a few miles of that base forty years later.

We faithfully held services every Sunday, normally on the gundeck, an open-air area in the forward part of the ship. We usually had no more than five or six of us all together, but we enjoyed what we had, and serving Christ together made us all stronger in the Lord. I think we also attended the base chapel and midweek Bible studies at the Christian serviceman's center.

Someone encouraged me not to judge all Filipinos by the vice and degradation I saw going on outside the Navy base, and I took that message to heart. I also remembered thinking about how nice it would be to travel to other parts of the Philippines and see how they lived. Looking back now, I can see that God was planting the seed of missions in my heart, even back then.

After five and-a-half months of touring the Pacific, it was time to head back to Pearl Harbor and the friends that I left had left behind there.

But first, it was time to go home and celebrate the Christmas holidays with my family.

CHAPTER 4

Still Sailing

I stayed for a month through the Christmas and New Year's holidays and well into January. This was the first time I had been home since Steve's wedding about nineteen months before and I had just been baptized in the Holy Spirit and left the CRC for the AG. The resulting switch had caused some unhappiness in my family, which I had not handled with great wisdom. One day, my dad surprised me when he said, "Dave, I know we have had some differences of opinion, but you are my son and I love you." This is the first time that I ever recall my dad saying he loved me. I do not remember what I said in response, but I was deeply touched and apologized for my part of the problem. We agreed to put aside our differences and focus on being father and son. The relationship has blossomed ever since, and Dad has always been supportive of my educational pursuits and ministry in the Assemblies of God. Debbie and I also visit their church from time to time when we are home. I have never forgotten that it was Dad, not me, who took the first step in healing the relationship.

I returned to Hawaii in January and life returned to normal. Six months later in June, 1978, my tour of duty in Hawaii was completed. At the same time, our ship was decommissioned and sold to the Taiwanese Navy. I had the honor of taking down the ship's American flag for the last time and ended up with my picture in a local Honolulu newspaper. Some months before, I was informed that my next duty station would the USS *Bowen*, a fast frigate, which is a destroyer type of ship, and was homeported in Charleston, South Carolina. I was pleased with the assignment and looked forward to the change of scenery, although I would miss Pearl Harbor; especially my church.

In looking back at this time over the years, this was a time of personal growth for me. In many respects, it was also a happy-go-lucky time where my responsibilities in life were minimal. As long as I did my job, the Navy was happy with me. I had a dry roof over my head and food in my stomach, as well as a twice monthly paycheck that was more than sufficient to meet my needs. I could not just resign from the Navy, but they could not easily fire me either. With these basic needs met, I was free to grow up, survive adolescence and enter adulthood. Spiritually, it was a time to grow and be discipled. While I was involved in the church's sound ministry and served as the Protestant lay leader on my ship, these were not heavy responsibilities—something that would radically change in the future.

After another thirty day leave in Grand Rapids, I arrived in Charleston nine days before the ship set sail for overseas. I had time to visit one church, (Glad Tidings Assembly of God, where I met some people who would later become my friends), before taking off for a part of the world I had never seen before—Latin America.

My new ship, the *Bowen* was much larger than the *Tawakoni*, although many considered a fast frigate to be a fairly small ship. It was 438 feet long, more than twice the length of the "Big T" and forty-six feet, nine inches across,[1] about nine feet wider than the Tawakoni. We had a crew of about 250 enlisted men and twenty, or so, officers. It was small enough to get to know everybody on board. The communication center where I worked was much larger than the *Tawakoni*'s and had radio equipment that I had not used before, but I made the adjustment with a minimum of difficulty. Like before, I eventually became the Protestant lay leader. The number of Christians on board was much smaller, percentage wise, than on the *Tawakoni*. When I complained to the Lord

---

[1] https://military.wikia.org/wiki/USS_Bowen_(FF-1079) (accessed April 27, 2020).

about it one day, he said, "Well, go make some disciples," reminding me of my responsibility to the Great Commission.

We left Charleston and, in company with two other Navy ships, headed for the south Atlantic, stopping first in Puerto Rico and then moving down the east coast of Latin America, stopping in many countries that had seaports. We eventually passed Cape Horn on the southern tip of South America and then made our way up the west coast, treading the waters of the eastern Pacific and stopping at many places along the way. Eventually, we passed through the Panama Canal, and then home to Charleston in December, 1978.

The trip was mainly for public relations, although we did do various exercises with some of the navies of Latin America. We also were required to open our ships to locals who wanted tours. In many places, we arrived to find that our coming had been announced in local newspapers, despite the Navy's policy about not announcing ships' movements. Hundreds of locals wanted to visit the ships. This was at the height of the Cold War where most of America's attention was focused elsewhere. Latin America was a political backwater then, so apparently the Navy was not too concerned about letting the locals know that we were coming.

A number of memories about this time stand out clearly in my mind. The first was my continued exposure to the Charismatic movement. I think it was in Rio de Janeiro, or Fortaleza, both in Brazil, that I had the opportunity to fellowship with a charismatic Anglican missionary. In Chile, I was surprised to discover that so many Methodists there were Pentecostal! At that time, I knew nothing of the history of the Pentecostal revival that had swept through the Methodists in Chile in the early 20th century, about the same time that revival broke out at the Azusa Street Mission, which would give birth to the Assemblies of God and a number of other Pentecostal groups in America. I remember attending a number of Pentecostal services in various churches there, including the Assemblies of God. I also met a Methodist Pentecostal missionary who was a graduate of Oral Roberts University in Tulsa, Oklahoma. I do not remember how I got connected with any of these people, but I do remember being impressed with the excitement of what God was doing there, even if I did not speak any Spanish. In at least one Assemblies of God church, I was given the opportunity to share a brief testimony from the pulpit because the people wanted to give me the opportunity to fulfill the Great Commission!

Since there were three ships travelling together as a small squadron, the Navy assigned a chaplain to make the cruise with us. Our ship carried a helicopter and its crew, and one of their duties was to ferry the chaplain, an ordained Methodist minister, from ship to ship whenever we were at sea on a Sunday. On those days, what we dubbed the "holy helo" dutifully brought the chaplain from ship to ship. While our ship had a helicopter landing pad, I do not think all of the others did, as I seem to recall the poor chaplain being lowered in a harness to the deck of at least one of the ships. Somehow, he survived it all in good humor.

I also did my share of sightseeing and exploring, but most of the memories have long faded. One bright spot was that not only was I able to stay in contact with my family by mail, although delivery was often erratic, I could also stay in contact by ship-to-shore telephone that the Navy arranged with ham operators in the States. However, doing it this way meant that only one person could speak at a time. As a trained Navy radioman, this was no problem for me, but it was a bit challenging for those we called who had no such experience with this type of communication. Nor was it private, so anything my family said would be heard by everyone in the communication center. Nevertheless, it did provide another connection to home, which we all deeply appreciated.

We returned to Charleston in December and I went home for a two week leave over the holidays. Once back in Charleston, I started attending Glad Tidings Assembly of God Church, which I had visited when I first came to Charleston, and I started making new friends. This church was much smaller than the church in Honolulu and only had services on Sundays and Wednesdays, so it was not quite the center of my life as First Assembly in Honolulu had been, but it still became a haven for me, a place where I could belong. The pastor, Reverend Ernie Oliver, and his wife, Ruth, became precious to me and remained in touch long after I left. Others became dear friends for that season of time. Here, my involvement in the church was mainly through helping on church workdays, which the church had regularly on Saturdays. I remember singing hymns as I scrubbed the baptismal tank or mowed the grass. In time, Pastor Oliver and his wife asked me to help give some pastoral care to military personnel that visited the church, which I was glad to do, but I do not recall that this ever developed into a large ministry.

I had never experienced Pentecostalism in the American South before and I was in for a few surprises. I had not yet studied the history of the Assemblies of God and was not aware that early Pentecostals frowned on just about anything considered to be fun, whether it was dancing, movies, bowling or long list of other things. Somehow, these behavioral standards never made it to California or Hawaii, or if they had, they had changed long before I arrived.

One of the forbidden activities was men and women going swimming together which was usually described somewhat incorrectly as "mixed bathing." One day, someone casually mentioned to me that Pastor Oliver opposed "mixed bathing." Thinking that he was talking about people who were not married to each taking showers together, I was horrified to think that any Christian could endorse such a thing. Fortunately, my friend clarified the matter, although Pastor Oliver himself never mentioned it, nor did he enforce it on us. Still, I decided it might not be wise to mention that our singles' group in Hawaii occasionally held beach parties!

Being from the North, I saw no problem with mowing the church grass in the summer wearing nothing more than cutoff shorts and shoes—and no one ever told me that Southern Pentecostals thought that was immodest. My wife and I were back in South Caroline thirty-five years later and looked up the Olivers, who by this time had retired and lived in the northern part of the state, and we shared a wonderful meal together. While reminiscing about old times and having good fellowship, Pastor Oliver admitted that I had changed his theology! It seems that one day he drove by the church while I was mowing the lawn without wearing a shirt. But he noticed that I was worshiping and praising the Lord while pushing the mower. He then concluded that maybe his views on modesty needed a bit of changing. Then I finally admitted to him that I had been involved in beach parties at the Honolulu church before coming to Charleston and we all had a good laugh.

While Honolulu had a good public transportation system, Charleston did not, and I needed to buy a car. As I prayed about it, I really felt like the Lord wanted me to have a new car and I began to talk about it with my friends at church. To me, what I drove was for utilitarian purposes and not a status symbol as it is for so many Americans. Nor did I care about material things in general. But in this case, I really believed that God wanted me to get a new car. So, I went shopping for one. I had enough money for a basic down payment but knew I would be making car payments for a while. Finally, I found a 1978 Plymouth Volare that had been used as a dealer demonstration model for a year. While it had 10,000 miles on it, it had never been purchased and was legally titled a new car. Since it fit my budget and the brand had a good reputation for quality, I bought it. With help from a generous gift from a friend, my down payment was much larger than I anticipated and I paid it off within two years—much earlier than I had expected. To date, this has been the only time God has ever spoken to me about buying a material item. Not only had I stepped out in faith in doing what I believed God had wanted me to do, I had chosen a really good car. That car lasted eleven years and went with me for my remaining time in the Navy, seven years of school and into my early years in full time ministry. No wonder God wanted me to have a new car. I would need it for a long time!

Like in Pearl Harbor, life in Charleston settled into a routine of executing my Navy duties and participating in the church. Since the church only had midweek services on Wednesday nights, unlike the church in Honolulu, I had to find other ways to occupy my free time. Since Charleston was an old Civil War town, I did a bit of sightseeing as well. I also had plenty of time to write or call my family. But like Hawaii, the Navy and church pretty much dominated my life.

In September, 1979, it was time for the *Bowen* to deploy overseas again, this time heading east into the Mediterranean. While the tour in South America had been primarily public relations, this tour was strictly no-nonsense military. The Soviet Navy patrolled both the Atlantic and the Mediterranean as we did, since the seas, by international law, were open to anybody. This part of the world was much closer to the Soviet Union and they had strong national interests there. The debate as to whether America or the Soviet Union had the biggest and strongest navy was endless. There was a certain level of tension in traversing this part of the world that I had not felt elsewhere, possibly because the Mediterranean is also a much smaller ocean than the Atlantic or Pacific. Thankfully, the Cold War never became a shooting war.

Life at sea during the deployment quickly settled into a different routine. The communication center had to be manned around the clock whether in port or at sea, due to the lack of Naval communication facilities on shore, so we were divided into three watch sections and I was the supervisor of my section. Our schedule was staggered so that we took turns working the late-night hours. Most other departments on the ship did the same at sea, but had a more normal schedule in port. To help cope with all the odd hours the crew was working, the cooks served four meals a day when we were at sea. In addition to breakfast, lunch and dinner, they served food at midnight, called "midrats," short for midnight rations, to serve those going on watch or coming off it in the middle of the night. Midrats consisted of leftovers from the previous meals, but it was enough for us to keep body and soul together.

Those cooks were amazing fellows. I think they knew at least forty-seven different ways to make roast beef! Apparently, the Navy was not overly generous with funds for food. Being at sea outside of the United States was also a big logistical challenge because it required taking on supplies from whatever sources were available whenever we pulled into a port. They really did the best they could, although some of the crew failed to appreciate their efforts. The main drinks were water, coffee and Kool-Aid, which we called bug juice because, even in the middle of the ocean, we could not get rid of the ever-spawning cockroaches.

Since we did not work or sleep every hour of the day, some limited forms of entertainment were in order. Every night the dining hall was turned into a theater, minus the soft drinks and popcorn. If the ship remained at sea for a while and it was not possible to get new movies, reruns became the order of the day. We also played cards, although except for an occasional Bingo night, (in which I did not participate) where the pot was split between the winner and a Navy charity, gambling was thankfully expressly prohibited. Moreover, being a classical bookworm, I had a fair number of books on board. I also may have been the only man in the Navy who was not a chaplain that had a small theological library right aboard the ship! I also wrote letters to my family, as well as using the same ship-to-shore calling system we had used on the previous cruise.

We spent all of our time in the western Mediterranean. For some reason, we were never ordered to go east of Italy, and when not actually at sea, spent most of our time visiting ports in Spain, France and Italy. As usual, most of the guys hit the bars. The other believers and I had no problem looking for other things to do, seeing what sites we could see, including the famous Leaning Tower of Pisa in Italy. We also enjoyed meals in strange restaurants in strange cities while trying not to get lost.

There were several events that stand out to me forty years later. Not all of them were positive. We were visiting Barcelona, Spain, on November 4, 1979, when Iranian revolutionaries overran the U.S.

Embassy in Teheran and took fifty-two American citizens hostage. While we were not among the ships sent from the Mediterranean to the Persian Gulf to deal with this crisis, the situation was tense, and became even more so when the Ayatollah Khomeini declared a special "kill an American day" while we were still in Barcelona. The captain wisely refused to let anyone leave the ship that day. Thankfully, the crisis was eventually resolved peacefully and all of the hostages were returned safely to American shores.

The second experience was a lot more fun. We spent the Christmas holidays in port in Livorno, northern Italy. One of the Filipinos onboard ship arranged an overnight tour to Rome and I joined the tour. We were able to visit places like the Coliseum and the Circus Maximus, although the tour guide could not confirm what church historians teach about Christians being put to death in these places. The high point of the tour, even for a non-Catholic like me, was a visit to Vatican and the opportunity to attend the annual Christmas Eve midnight mass there. I actually took a photo of Pope John Paul II as he walked down the center aisle no more than fifteen or twenty feet from me!

The third memorable event happened a couple of months later. While we were visiting the beautiful city of Palermo, Sicily, an island just off the Italian boot, we received orders to leave immediately and head for the coast of Tunisia, North Africa, just south of Sicily. It seems that nearby Libya was threatening the Tunisian Mediterranean oilfields, and the Navy was asked to help maintain the peace. It was the only time in my naval career where we sailed under potential wartime conditions.

Fortunately, the situation calmed down after a few days, and we then pulled into the port of Tunis for a few days. This was my first, and to date, the only country I have visited in Africa. Also, while I may have met some Muslims in the past, this was my first exposure to Islam—about which I knew nothing at the time. I would like to say that I took an avid interest in learning more about their country, culture and religion but, alas, the truth must come out. The only memory I have of our visit is going to a restaurant in a large hotel and being shocked at having to pay a whole dollar for a can of Coca-Cola! Obviously, my sensitivity to, and interest in, Muslims was still in the future.

Finally, it was time to head home. We arrived in Charleston on a cold, rainy day, April 3, 1980, my 23rd birthday. Like some of the other guys, I headed for the airport for a couple of weeks in Michigan with my family. We did not stay in Charleston long. The ship was scheduled for a complete overhaul, including repairs and updating of various shipboard systems. To accomplish this, the ship had to be completely taken out of the water and placed in a drydock. In a drydock, the ship floats into the drydock and then the water is drained out below the dock. The ship must then be secured in such a way that it remains in place and does not tip over. To do this we were sent to the Old Brooklyn Navy Yard in New York City and remained there for about a year.

New York City was a fun place to visit with lots of things to do and see, including many historical sites like the Statue of Liberty and the Empire State Building. Some places gave free admission to military personnel and I was able to see off Broadway shows and even Major League Baseball games at no cost. But the first thing I did was go looking for a church. As it turned out, there was an Assemblies of God church within a few blocks from where our ship was located. I discovered that this church was the original Teen Challenge, a global, Christ-centered program of the AG for getting people get off drugs and other addictions. Teen Challenge had been founded by a pastor named David Wilkerson back in the 1950s.

I did not go alone. One day I met a sailor named Glenn Yankle, whose ship was also in drydock near ours. He was a charismatic Lutheran and we became inseparable. Through Glenn, I came into contact with yet another strand of the Charismatic Movement, Lutheran charismatics. He had become involved with a group who went to their own respective Lutheran churches on Sunday morning, but since the Lutheran churches did not have night services, they would gather in one of the churches for a charismatic prayer meeting. Every Sunday night they met in a different place. One day, I got the bright idea to see if they would like to have one of the meetings on our ship! They agreed, and so did my commanding officer. Glenn helped me host them for an outdoor prayer meeting on the helo deck. Fortunately, the weather was nice and we had a good time.

Meanwhile, my younger brother, Tom, had graduated from high school and joined the Navy also. Like me, he became a radioman. The Navy had a policy that brothers could apply to serve at the same duty station together, as long as it met the needs of the Navy. Tom applied, knowing full well that my enlistment was coming to an end. He was approved, and Glenn and I picked him up at the airport just before the July 4th holiday. Unwittingly, however, we encountered a small problem. By this time, I was the leading radioman and in charge of the communication center. While I did my best to not show favoritism to Tom, some of the guys inevitably complained. When a new crewman came aboard, he was expected at some point to spend ninety days helping the cooks and scrubbing pots and pans, no matter what his job classification was. When our boss noticed what was happening, he solved the problem by sending poor Tom to take his turn in working with the cooks. But at least we enjoyed being together.

During this time, I also went through a personal crisis. While home for Christmas in 1977, I had dated and fallen in love with a young lady who was part of the church that Steve and Terrie attended. We continued the relationship by long distance and became engaged in late 1978 and planned to marry when I got out. While I was in New York, however, she called off the engagement. I was deeply hurt. But out of the ashes of my broken heart and shattered dreams, God brought a young couple into my life that would speak God's direction to me, even though they were not aware of it. Ever since my days in San Diego, I knew that God had a call on my life to ministry. I did not know what kind of ministry, nor did I know where, nor did I know if it would be full-time, but I was trusting that God would show me when the time came. This couple shared that he had just completed his freshman year at a place called Central Bible College, an Assemblies of God Bible college in Springfield, Missouri. He told me it was a good education and that it was inexpensive. I became interested, and soon got an application form and began to pray for God's direction. Meanwhile, God used all of these friends, especially Glenn and Tom, to pour healing balm on my hurting heart and help me to forgive her.

Finally, the day came for my release from the Navy. While the actual date of my release from the Navy was October 8, I had some unused leave time so I was able to go home for good around September 1, just in time to join my family in celebrating the annual Labor Day holiday. Five years in the Navy had given me the chance to transition from adolescence to adulthood, travel the world and meet people I would likely have never met any other way. I had participated in ministry as well as I could while in the service and now the time had come to fully prepare to answer God's call.

CHAPTER 5

Central Bible College

When I arrived home in Grand Rapids, I moved back into my parents' home and was still uncertain as to my next step in life. The first thing I needed to find was a church, and at least a temporary job. Because I had not grown up in the Assemblies of God, I had no roots in any of the churches in the area. I decided to start by visiting First Assembly of God (now simply called Grand Rapids First Church), which I had visited a couple of years before when I was home on leave. I decided to go to this church again, and then check out the other AG churches in the area. But I enjoyed First Assembly so much that I never even visited the other churches until much later, when I was invited to speak in them. Nearly four decades have now passed, most of which were spent outside of Grand Rapids, and this church remains my home church to this day.

I then found a job in a business that packed industrial equipment for shipping overseas. From the beginning, I told them I might not be there long, and that was no problem for them. They were also kind enough to allow me to delay a week in starting because my dad needed my help in putting a new roof on the house. In truth, the new job required a lot of mechanical work, which is not my strength. I was not well-suited for the job, but I hung in there, knowing that it might be temporary. Since this company was not far from where my dad worked, we shared the ride and had some good times together.

Meanwhile, God confirmed his call on my life when Central Bible College (CBC) accepted me as a new student to start in the January, 1981, term. I was excited about going to college. Because of my military service, I qualified for a monthly stipend from the government to help cover the costs of education. I had never been to Springfield, Missouri before, but after five years of touring the world with the Navy, this was not a problem. I immediately felt at home on campus, although I was a bit of a "duck out of the water." At the age of 23, I was already older than most of the seniors, and I had already seen more of the world than most people see in a lifetime. After living for five years with men who used the name of Jesus as a curse word, the godly campus atmosphere was refreshing. It was at least six months before I realized that not everything at CBC was perfect!

Springfield sits on a plateau in the Ozark mountains and had a unique cultural subset that was a mixture of southern, rural and mountain folk. One CBC faculty member once aptly described it as a city "where 140,000 farmers lived together." The campus sat on thirty-two acres of land on the city's north side. There was one main building where most of the classes were held, as well as the main administrative and most of the faculty offices. There were four dormitories, two gymnasiums, a cafeteria, a large library and a chapel that comprised the main buildings on campus. I was assigned a room in Welch Hall, the oldest men's dorm. Unlike the newer dorms, our dorm had community bathrooms on each hall. While this meant less privacy, some of the guys actually preferred Welch because sharing a bathroom meant having more fellowship! I would have been happy wherever they put me.

I went to the library to study immediately after the first day of classes, and fully expected to see a lot of other students there, but I was quite surprised to see that I had the library to myself! Obviously, I had a lot to learn about campus life. The library did not start to be filled up until the second or third week of classes. On the other hand, I had come to CBC to get serious about pursuing God's call on my life, and I never felt bad about spending much, much more time in the library than the gym or the student union. Back when I was in high school, my only motivation for study had been to stay eligible for sports, and my grades reflected that attitude. Now, with greater maturity, an expanded worldview and an eternal purpose for life, I attacked my studies with great zeal. I also got involved in campus ministries, and even spent the first summer serving a church on a Native American reservation in western Washington state.

Springfield had more than fifty Assemblies of God churches, and many of them sent buses to CBC to pick up students who attended them. While I had a car, I did not have a lot of money, so I rode the church bus to enjoy fellowship with others and to save on gas. One day in my second semester, I went down to get on a church bus and saw a friend who was going to another church. He pointed out his church's bus, and it was truly something to behold. Along with the typical yellow, it was painted in several colors with words like "Glory Land Express" proudly emblazoned on the front. Reflecting Springfield's rural flavor, the bus driver was wearing a cowboy hat, boots and blue jeans on a Sunday morning! I said to my friend, "This I have to see," and climbed on board with him.

The church, Mount Calvary Assembly of God, was located about fifteen miles east of town, and the people who attended were warm-hearted country folks. As I sat in a pew that morning, I had the strange sense that the Holy Spirit had something for me at this church, although I had no clue as to what that might be. I decided to keep going to that church, and a week later, I was asked to become the church's youth director. At this point I had not had much experience in any kind of ministry, let alone ministry to youth, and yet I accepted because the Spirit of God was drawing me in that direction. I stayed at that church until my graduation from CBC. I served as the youth director for about a year-and-a-half, then remained as an unpaid associate pastor for another couple of years, and I gained a lot of valuable ministry experience in other areas as well.

One day, an evangelist from the deep South visited our church for a week of revival meetings. He announced proudly that he had never been to Bible college and was a graduate of the "school of hard knocks" and the "college of the Holy Ghost." His sincerity was evident and I did not doubt his calling. He had us doing Jericho marches around the sanctuary and long, good altar calls. In some services there was no preaching, which some thought was great. When he did preach, I found his exposition of the biblical text to be quite shallow. I am not a critical person by nature, but at a time when I was checking out various ministries, and considering what ministry God had in mind for me, I was disappointed with what I saw. I told the Lord that if this is what the ministry of the evangelist was like, I was not interested. I told the Lord that if he ever called me to be an evangelist, I would focus on the preaching of the Word. A few years later, he would remind me of that promise.

I excelled academically. I loved my classes, my instructors and my classmates. I invested most of my life either in class, chapel, the library, and on the weekends, the church. I developed a lot of good friendships, several of which continued long after I graduated. During my second semester in the fall of 1981, I began to get involved in Campus Missions Fellowship, which focused on special Friday night services where missionaries from all over the world came and shared their hearts, telling us what God was doing in the far-flung regions of the world. We had long lingering altar calls where we prayed for the needs of the world, and allowed the Holy Spirit to search our hearts regarding our roles in world evangelism.

While I was home in 1980 after getting out of the Navy, I renewed my relationship with the young lady that had called off our engagement. The relationship continued into 1982 and we again planned to marry. Again, she called off the relationship, this time only fifteen days before the wedding. This time, the reason she gave was she knew that I had a call on my life to ministry and she did not want to hold me back. In truth, she had always been honest about that fact that she did not feel a call to ministry, but I did not see that as a problem as long as she was willing to support me—which, for a while, it seemed like she would. Looking back, she made the right decision. She saw more clearly than I did that both spouses need to feel a call to the ministry. It was a painful lesson to learn, and the final breakup hurt for a long time, but God eventually mended my heart. In time I dated other ladies, but many years would pass before I would meet the love of my life.

Meanwhile, school and ministry continued as I grew deeper in my relationship with the Lord, and prepared for whatever ministry he had for me. I loved the godly environment with people of like-minded faith and interests. I spent hours with my friends discussing what we had learned in classes and what we felt that God was speaking to us about the Bible, theology, missions and other forms of ministry. Godly instructors guided us and modelled godly lifestyles, and ministry perspectives, both in and out of the classroom. One friend, Pat Fee, a Virginia native who was also a military veteran, asked me to share an apartment with him off campus, and we ended up being roommates for about two-and-a-half years. We had a lot of good times together.

By this time, I was not only studying and doing ministry, I was working a part-time job delivering newspapers morning and evening. It was a motor route inside the city of Springfield. I had also felt led by the Lord to go back and join the Navy Reserve for three years to augment my income. This meant spending one weekend a month in training, with two weeks active duty somewhere every year. I stayed in the Reserves until a few months after graduation.

Something happened in the fall of 1982 that changed my future. The Campus Missions Fellowship announced that they would be offering partial scholarships for those that agreed to go on a missionary assignment, either at home or abroad, the following summer. God began to speak to me about applying. I had planned to remain in Springfield the next summer and go to summer school, as well carrying on with everything else. But the Holy Spirit would not leave me alone. After three weeks of being under the conviction of the Holy Spirit, I was absolutely miserable. Finally, I gave in and told God I would go, and peace returned to my heart.

The next question was, "Where would I go?" I had a burden for China at the time, and was supporting some ministry there, so I went to the Assemblies of God headquarters right there in Springfield and inquired about ministry in China. China was not really open at that time, except for Hong Kong. The missionaries in Hong Kong were asking for summer interns to help in hotel ministries, as many churches met in these places, as well as occasional day trips across the border into mainland China. When I prayed about it, I just did not sense that the Lord was leading me there. I then asked if there were other openings in countries near China. The gentleman who interviewed me told me that there was a missionary in the Philippines named Dwight Palmquist, who was looking for interns who would help with pioneer preaching, literature distribution and church planting. When I heard this, I sensed that this was God's direction for me and I was accepted to go.

Meanwhile, school continued as well as ministry, and now, fundraising for the summer trip. The months ground on as God continued to work in my life through long hours of study, ministry, work and the Friday night missions' service. But finally, it was time to head to Asia. I had no idea that the next eight weeks would change my life.

As it turned out, there were four of us interns, two guys and two gals. All of us were students at AG colleges, and one of them had been with me at CBC. We ended up forming a team under the leadership of a local pastor, Reverend Eli Gaad, whom Dwight had arranged to be our team leader. Our flights were arranged so that we met in Los Angeles and traveled to the Philippines together. Since I had been to the Philippines before, I did not feel like it was a totally strange place, although I had never been to Manila, which is where we landed.

After a couple of days in Manila to get oriented by Dwight and get over a bit of our jetlag, three of us, along with Pastor Gaad, who I would later come to regard as my Filipino father, took off for the provinces. One of the women stayed behind to do ministry in Manila. When I had visited the Philippines six years previously, I had wondered how Filipinos in other parts of the country lived. I was about to find out.

We traveled twelve hours south of Manila by bus to the Bicol region. This region is comprised of six provinces, and encompasses the southern third of the main island, Luzon. We began in the city of Tabaco. We spent about a week there helping in a church planting crusade. We brought a film projector with us and showed the Campus Crusade's *Jesus*—one of the most powerful and accurate films on the life of Christ ever made, in my opinion. My job was to run the projector and help in other ways. That church was to become one of the leading Assemblies of God churches in that region for a number of years. The pastor, Jesse Tan, would become a good friend. In total, we probably spent about a month traveling through the region. While we did no preaching at the crusade in Tabaco, because they already had a speaker, we did plenty of it in other places. At one point, we covered ten communities in eighteen days, hauling our suitcases, film equipment and other things around by commercial transportation, normally non-airconditioned buses. It was hot, sweaty and dirty travel, but we did not mind most of the time. This was, however, at least one exception. One night, I was sleeping in a room over a church sanctuary with one other guy. It was hot and stuffy, with only one fan that we shared. I complained to God about it, stating that I could have spent the summer in my air-conditioned apartment in Springfield, the Lord rebuked me saying, "Who are you to determine where you will go and how you will live?" This was not the only time I had to repent and change my attitude, but it was a lesson I never forgot. We were serving the Lord and leading people to Christ, and gaining valuable missionary experience along the way. I had no idea how much this part of the Philippines would become so important to my life in the future.

From there, we took a bus north to Lucena City, which was located in a province only about four hours south of Manila. There we boarded a passenger ferry for an overnight trip to Tablas Island in the central part of the country known as the Visayas Region. There, the fourth member of the team joined us from Manila and brought a Filipino friend with her. Pastor Gaad, our team leader, was from this island and had planted the first AG church on the island in 1957, the year I was born. He had three brothers who had gone into the ministry, and two of them were still living on Tablas. One of his brothers, Eddie, had taken over the church Pastor Gaad had pioneered. Pastor Eddie owned a jeepney, a common form of transportation in the Philippines. The original design came from WWII U.S. Army jeeps that were left after the war. The Filipinos added a riding compartment in the back where passengers sit facing each other. To this day, it remains a popular form of transportation.

While Pastor Eddie supplemented his living by driving his jeep commercially, he also made it available to our team for the outreaches that we held on the island, saving us the trouble of changing from one vehicle to another. On the back of the jeepney, there were two small ladders to the top, since jeepneys often carried the cargo, baggage and people on the roof. I often chose to ride up there, sitting in the wheel well of the spare tire that was positioned toward the front of the jeepney. In actuality, it really was not a smart move but, as a young person, I still had more energy than common sense. Had the driver needed to stop suddenly, or if there had been a head-on collision, I could have been thrown off the roof and seriously injured. Thank the Lord that nothing ever happened.

I opted to take the risk because it afforded me a panoramic view of the people, the towns and the rice fields that we passed on this rural, largely undeveloped island. It also gave me the opportunity to dream. I began to see possibilities about what God might use me to do if he were to call me as a missionary to the Philippines. I could see the needs of the Filipinos for a relationship with Christ and I saw the possibilities of me conducting outreaches, leading thousands of people to Christ and planting churches all over the country. I did not know at that point that God would call me to that work, but I could not help but ask the question, "What if?"

After eight weeks, it was time to say goodbye to the Philippines and head home. We had held outreaches in many communities and I had preached twenty-nine times in eight weeks. We had seen many indicate their desire to follow Jesus, and we had worked with pastors eager to reach their communities for Christ. Once again, my worldview had been challenged and expanded.

Up to this point, I had been at CBC for over two and-a-half years. During this time, I had consistently sought God's direction regarding my future ministry, but he had chosen to be silent. As I entered my senior year at CBC, my prayers were about to be radically answered, sending me in a direction that I did not exactly expect.

As the fall 1983 term of my senior year at CBC began, I started to sense that God was speaking to me to get a master's degree from the Assemblies of God Graduate School, which was also in Springfield, so I began to focus my studies in that direction. (The Graduate School changed its name to the Assemblies of God Theological Seminary (AGTS) the year I enrolled). Meanwhile, I continued faithfully participating in the Friday night missionary services. By this time, I had given up my paper route, but I continued in the Navy Reserve, and was still active in church, although I was no longer the youth director. With the senior year there came a couple of nice social events, such as the senior retreat and senior banquet, and I participated with gusto. But, as usual, the lion's share of my time was invested in my studies and I continued to do well.

That fall of 1983, we had our annual missions' convention. While I enjoyed the services, the most powerful experience I had that week actually happened when I went to bed one night. While lying there waiting to fall asleep the presence of God came upon me in a mighty way.

In that moment, God began to speak to my heart about the masses of people outside of the United States who had never heard the gospel. That night, I accepted God's call to be a missionary, and my future began to come into sharper focus. While God did not specifically mention any country or the part of the world where I was to go, it was clear in my mind that God was pointing me to Southeast Asia.

But God was not finished yet. Although it was not clear for some time, God began to move me in the direction as to which type of ministry I would engage in after AGTS, and would continue to shape the first nineteen years of my missionary career. I think it was about January, 1984, that we had a spiritual emphasis week. The Spirit moved in a mighty way in these meetings. One night stands out clearly in my mind. The service began around 7 p.m., and during the praise and worship time, the Holy Spirit fell upon us in an incredible way. We began to move towards the altar long before the speaker had the opportunity to preach. One young lady danced in the Spirit for about four hours, weaving around the rest of us who were standing or kneeling in prayer and worship. About 11:30 that night, the altar time subsided and the evangelist said he was not sure what he should do. Someone encouraged him to preach the message he had prepared, and so he did.

After those meetings, I noticed that my heart had changed about the ministry of the evangelist. I had seen a great example of how God could move in a wonderful way in altar calls that did not exclude the solid preaching of the Word. Then, I began to hear something from the Spirit that I never expected to hear. I sensed that God was leading me to engage in an evangelistic ministry. Since I knew that the Lord was leading me to continue my education at AGTS, I just assumed that I would do evangelism on the weekends while I was in seminary, and then move on towards my calling in missions, which, at that time, required a couple of years of pastoral ministry to meet the qualifications to become a missionary. I had no idea how wrong I was.

Finally, it was time to graduate. For three and-a-half years, including summer sessions, godly teachers and administrators had poured themselves into me and my classmates' lives in the classroom, chapel, the missions' services and in every other way. I owed them an unpayable debt. We, at the same time, had worked hard, attended the classes, done our homework and passed the tests, along with doing ministry. We had been challenged and stretched in ways we would not have been otherwise. Graduation that May, although mixed with a bit of sadness for saying farewell to many that I had come to love, was a joyous celebration. As my parents, Steve, my older brother, his wife Terrie, and Vicky, their newborn daughter, and families of my classmates, all gathered in Springfield to celebrate the occasion, a new chapter of my life was about to begin.

CHAPTER 6

The Assemblies of God
Theological Seminary

After graduation from CBC, I made two overseas trips before beginning my studies at AGTS. First, I joined my Navy Reserve unit for two weeks of training at the Naval Communications Station in Nea Makri, Greece, which is on the Aegean Sea about twenty-two miles northeast of Athens. We went there for training because if the U.S. Armed Forces had ever needed to be totally mobilized for war, this is where we would have been sent. While we were there, we took the opportunity to do some touring. We saw the Acropolis in Athens, and I stood on Mar's Hill, the very same place where the apostle Paul had debated the Athenian philosophers in Acts 17. I also visited the ancient market area where he had preached Christ. We also went to see the ruins of ancient Corinth, about fifty-two miles south of Athens. Again, I walked where Paul had walked. It was an amazing experience. My time in Greece was also my last official act with the Navy. My enlistment in the Naval Reserve was finished at the end of the trip and I felt the Lord telling me not to reenlist.

About a week after returning to Springfield, I took off for the Philippines for another eight weeks of ministry, in fulfillment of what I now knew to be God's call. Some details of this journey have faded from memory. I do remember spending three of those weeks on the island of Palawan, a long pencil-thin island in the southwestern part of the Philippines. I also believe that I went back to Romblon for more ministry with Pastor Gaad. The ministry was the same: evangelistic outreaches using gospel films, preaching and praying for people in altar calls. I loved it!

After returning to the States and squeezing in a couple of weeks in Michigan with my family, I was ready for my new adventure in studying at the graduate level. My classmates, on average, were a bit older than me. By this time, I was 27 years old, about four years younger than the median age of the student body. Many already had several years of ministry experience. A lot of them were also married. I also appreciated that some of my classmates from CBC also enrolled in AGTS, so I had some friends there when I first arrived. In fact, even two of my professors from CBC also moved to AGTS that same year.

Two other changes occurred the same time. Since I knew that God was calling me to evangelism on the weekends, I felt that my time at Mount Calvary had come to a close. I also wanted to attend a church in town where there were single people my age on the Sundays when I was not preaching. I ended up changing to Praise Assembly of God on Springfield's north side. I also wanted to move closer to AGTS, hopefully close enough to walk to school. In my senior year at CBC, I met a guy named Joshua Yang, who had come there to take some classes that were pre-requisites to getting into AGTS. We agreed to room together.

The house we rented was like no other house I have lived in, before or since. It was located in an older, somewhat rundown neighborhood near AGTS. It was a two-story house, with a separate entrance to the upstairs. It also had a long, somewhat dilapidated, wrap-around porch that was tilted to the right. If there was ice on the porch in the winter, there was always the possibility of sliding into the bushes! Inside, the furnace that heated the house actually sat right in the living room. When it kicked in during the winter months, it was so loud that no conversation was possible in the room. The house was so poorly insulated, that in winter, we could see our breath when standing in the kitchen. This was not a problem as we did not spend much time there anyway. To compensate for the poor insulation, we used a space heater in our rooms.

To top it off, the bathroom had an old claw-footed bathtub, but no shower. Having grown up in such a situation, it was no problem for me, but I am not sure that Josh was too thrilled. No sane man with a wife would have wanted to live there, but it was okay for a couple of bachelors.

We took the house because the rent was only $130.00 a month, which I think was below average, and about the only place nearby that fit our budgets. On top of that, the landlady's son owned a duplex next door. For some reason, he needed to use our outside water faucets to water the grass at the duplex. He insisted on paying a generous part of our utilities, and of course, we had no objections. Josh graduated with his Master of Arts degree in about a year and left. Tim Samorajski, one of our classmates, took his place. I had great relationships with both of them.

At this time, AGTS occupied part of the 5th, and all of the 6th floor of the distribution center of the Gospel Publishing House, the publishing arm of the AG, which was located in the Assemblies of God headquarters complex in downtown Springfield. The school later moved to its own location in another part of the city. Like I had done at CBC, I set up camp in the library and stayed there the whole three years.

I enrolled in the Master of Divinity program with a specific concentration in missions. This was critical to me because I had only taken one course in missions at CBC. Now that I knew what God was calling me to do, I wanted to focus my studies in that direction. I took as many courses as I could about missions. Here, I discovered the beauty of higher education. I learned that the higher I went in education, the more I could specialize in areas that were important to me. This would become even more true when I got to the doctoral level years later.

But while missions was my main interest, it was not the only one. I also had a keen desire to study the Old Testament. For example, I really did not understand the relationship between law and covenant, as expressed in books like Deuteronomy, and the role of the prophetical books. Taking courses in Old Testament theology allowed me to probe these questions. Since I had studied Greek at CBC, I decided to study a year of Hebrew at AGTS. The result was that I did not really become a master of either of them. Looking back, it might have been better to take more courses in Greek and really become proficient in that language. It would be one of the few missteps, if one could call it that, in my educational journey.

Because the academic load is much heavier at the graduate level, and because I wanted to make sure I had the time to absorb the lessons taught, I chose to take less hours almost every semester, although I needed to take enough to be considered a full-time student to continue to receive the benefits from the G.I. Bill. I took summer classes to make sure that I could graduate on time, and the plan actually worked quite well.

However, I did have one curious experience that happened every semester from the day I started CBC all the way through my last semester at AGTS. Every semester without exception, usually about the third week, it would dawn on me how much work there was to do, and I would begin to think, "Oh Lord, I can't do this!" and I would begin to slide into panic mode. Then, miraculously, I would look at the academic requirements and the calendar, and map out a study plan to make sure that everything was done on time. Then, I would spend the rest of the semester working my plan, and with few exceptions, it went well.

It was at AGTS that I began to grasp the fundamentals of missionary philosophy and how one could go about succeeding in missionary work. It was here that I began to study things like the concept of the indigenous church, meaning for the church to really take root in the soil of any culture it had to propagate, support and govern itself, without undue assistance from the outside. Later, I would learn that understanding these concepts—and actually applying them— were not necessarily the same thing. I also learned that applying them would take a lot of prayer, wisdom and patience. Neither could I have understood at the time, that to a great extent, my success or failure in applying these principles would depend on the strength of my relationships with local Filipino pastors.

Another major area of study within missions is understanding the role of culture in missions, and how to live and minister in another culture. Part of that included how to understand the gospel itself in a cross-cultural situation. And we were taught how to bring people to a relationship with Christ within their own cultural context, without compromising the gospel message in the process. This is not as easy as it might seem. Because of the broad complexity of cultures in today's world, AGTS could not provide all the answers to every situation, but they could, and did, teach me what questions to ask. As I would later discover, learning how to do this task well would be part and parcel of missionary life that takes place over the process of time.

Since God had begun leading me into evangelism during my last semester at CBC, I had started contacting local pastors to set up preaching engagements. Springfield has a lot of AG churches, but there were also a lot of AG ministers living in Springfield, with a lot more passing through on a regular basis. Consequently, local pastors got a lot of calls, and they had no reason to take a student like me all that seriously. I discovered that patience and persistence were necessary virtues in going about this task. I decided to get a part time job through an employment agency, just until I could schedule enough meetings to financially survive. I did get a job and worked for a week or two, but the Holy Spirit really dealt with me to not work, but to pursue my studies and the ministry. I was to trust and obey. I went through some lean times financially, but God took care of me.

I knew a few of the pastors in town because my work in the youth ministry at Mount Calvary, and because some of my CBC and AGTS classmates were pastoring small churches in the area. I also had a friend from CBC, Jimmy Davis, who graduated about a year ahead of me and was now on the evangelistic field as well as studying at AGTS. He shared with me that whenever he spoke for a pastor, he would then ask the pastor for references to other pastors that they knew, and get permission to use their name when calling other pastors. He also gave me some contacts to call. I took Jimmy's advice and began following the same method. In fact, I tried to make it easier for pastors by bringing along the AG church directory and just having the pastors for whom I preached just look through the directory and put their initials besides the names of the pastors they knew. Most were quite willing to do so and, slowly but surely, I began to fill the calendar and build up a new list of friends among the pastors, mostly within a four-hour drive of Springfield. With opportunities like this, I really had the opportunity to develop my preaching skills.

After my first year of seminary, which included one or two summer sessions, once again I was able to raise the money for summer ministry in the Philippines. Because of the summer sessions, I only stayed in the Philippines for five weeks. There were a couple of other interns in our group. This, time, Pastor Gaad did not travel with us because he was pioneering a church in Metro Manila. This time, we spent our time in provincial areas north of Manila. We even made a trip to Baguio City, where I had visited back in my Navy days and where, at the time of this writing, my wife and I currently reside. There, I met AG missionaries Steve and Linda Long. We stayed in their home for about three days and helped paint a Sunday school room in a local church.

Before the end of my first year at AGTS, much to my surprise, I was elected to serve as the vice-president of the Student Advisory Council (SAC) for the following year. I had done my best to make friends, but I had no idea that my colleagues thought that I was worthy to hold such a position. I was honored to serve. The year before, the previous SAC had started a student ministries program by endorsing a student who wanted to begin developing one. This year, the SAC took responsibility for the program and I got the job. We launched a preaching ministry in local churches, rest home visitation, etc. For the first few weeks, I did not get much time in the library because I was busy getting these ministries organized.

Later that year, I became heavily involved in the school's fundraising phone-a-thon and won the award for making the most phone calls. If we raised a certain number of pledges, that actually came in, we received a free hour of tuition. I ultimately earned several free credit hours.

I did manage to get to the library and got caught up on my studies, although it meant a lot of late nights. About this time, my new roommate, Tim, and I joined the YMCA and enjoyed working out about three times a week, although it did not stop my slowly expanding waistline. At the same time, I kept plodding forward with my weekend evangelistic ministry.

In April 1986, I experienced another momentous event in my life when was ordained into the ministry at the annual council of the Southern Missouri District of the Assemblies of God. There are three levels of ministerial recognition in the Assemblies of God, and ordination is the highest level. Back in 1983, shortly before I went to the Philippines on the trip that changed my life, I received the first level of credentials, which was then known as a Christian Worker's permit. A year later, I received my license to preach. Two years at the licensing level were required before ordination. At all levels, a written test, oral interview and personal references were required.

As they did for my CBC and graduation, and as they would do for my AGTS graduation the following year, my faithful parents came down to be a part of the meeting. At the ordination service, all candidates were invited to come forward to the altar for the laying on of hands by the leadership, which was an important part of the ceremony. Spouses were also asked to come and kneel behind the kneeling ordination candidate. I think I was the only single person ordained that year. While I was kneeling, I felt someone's hand on my back. I turned just a bit to see who was there to discover that my dear mother had taken it upon herself to take the place of where my wife would have been had I been married. I was really blessed, and the act of ordination was an amazing spiritual experience that I have never forgotten.

Once again, at the end of the school year, I was privileged to travel overseas. This time, I went to Singapore, a tiny city-state just off the tip of the Malay Peninsula in Southeast Asia. Earlier in the school year, I met a missionary to Singapore, Irvin Rutherford, and asked him if he might be interested in having me come to Singapore in the summer of 1986, and he graciously invited me. As it turns out, he was recruiting a lot of short-term volunteers to come to Singapore for a week or two of training. Then they would be sent elsewhere in Southeast Asia for ministry. Finally, they would return to Singapore for a short time before returning home. In my case, however, he opted to keep me in Singapore. He booked me to speak in churches, youth groups and even a couple of church camps, both of which were held in nearby Malaysia. He also had me teach a short leadership course that was already prepared. I had a class of exactly two students, who were fun to teach.

Singapore was, and continues to be, a beautiful city with one of the highest living standards in all of Asia. All of the world's major religions were well represented in Singapore. Therefore, I decided to request permission from AGTS to do an independent study course in Asian religions while there. It was just as well that I did so, because most of my speaking engagements were at night, so this gave me something worthwhile to do during the day. I often went by bus to the National University of Singapore whose library was open to outsiders. When I was outside the library, I had the opportunity to see these Asian religions in practice. For example, an annual tradition known as "The Month of the Hungry Ghost" occurred while I was there. I watched Buddhists burn food, paper money, paper homes, paper cars and all sorts of other things. This was done to care for the spirits of those who died but have no living relatives to venerate them in traditional ancestor rites. The fear is that if these hungry spirits are not cared for properly, they will bring curses upon the living. It gave me some great insights into their worldview, and I was reminded that the task of world evangelism remains unfinished.

I spent quite a bit of time alone, which put a bit of a damper on the summer for me. Throughout the summer, I actually questioned whether God had really called me to go that summer, or just allowed me to go because he knew I really wanted to go. On the outside, the time did not seem as fruitful as the summers in the Philippines, but God judges by a different standard. Whatever the answer to these questions might have been, God certainly did a work in my life that summer by expanding my view of missions beyond the Philippines. At my request, Irvin wrote a letter of endorsement for me and sent it to the Division of Foreign Missions (DFM)[1] at the AG headquarters in Springfield. He also suggested that as long as I was living in Springfield, it would be a good idea to visit the DFM, introduce myself to the leadership and let them know that I would be applying for appointment after a couple of years of ministry. It was a great suggestion that I did follow through on when I returned. That visit, as well as Irwin's letter, would guide me in a manner that I did not expect, nor initially like, but sort of directed me in my ministry in the years immediately following graduation from AGTS.

In the meantime, I had one more year of school to go. Like the year before, I served on the SAC, although not without reservation. I thought seriously about not allowing my name to stand for reelection because I thought of some other things I wanted to do. In the end, I allowed my name to stand because I felt, both then and now, that some continuity of leadership from one year to the next would be good for the student body. Because the student council president had repeatedly predicted that I would follow him as president because I was the vice-president, I assumed that would be the case. But that is not what happened. Our procedure was to have the student body elect who would be on the council, and then the council members would vote among themselves who would hold what post. To my surprise, someone else was elected president, and I was selected to be just a student representative. I was somewhat disappointed, and the departing president, who conducted the

---

[1] The name was changed to Assemblies of God World Missions in 2001.

vote among the council members, was absolutely shocked. However, I told him that there is no such thing as a demotion when one is serving the Lord, although I wasn't totally sure I was convinced of it myself. Since the actual election took place before I went to Singapore for the summer, I thought seriously that summer about resigning, especially since I had reservations about allowing my name to stand in the first place. Quitting, fortunately, is not in my nature. While I had some rough spots along the way, we had a good year and I was glad I stuck it out.

Again, it was a great academic year for me. Like at CBC, godly professors poured their lives and knowledge into me and my classmates, both in and out of the classroom. As usual, I buried myself in the library, although by my second year, I actually spent a lot of time studying in the SAC office, which was adjacent to the library. Even then, however, I regularly toured the library to visit with my friends and look for study materials. Also, by this time, I was taking a lot of my evening meals in the headquarters' cafeteria. It was more convenient than going home to eat, and not that much more expensive. It also gave me more time with my friends. In fact, many of my "library tours" were to invite my classmates to join me for dinner. I developed a number of good friendships with both male and female students, some of which have continued to bless my life throughout the years since then.

In the fall of that year I made good on Irvin Rutherford's suggestion that I visit the leadership of the DFM just to introduce myself. I went to see the director of personnel, Ron Iwasko, who I actually knew from church. I went into the meeting thinking that I would just get better acquainted with him and review my qualifications for missionary service, just to see if I was missing anything. I also wanted them to know that I was interested in becoming a missionary. At the end of the meeting, I asked him what he thought, and was shocked when he said he was tempted to take me aboard as a missionary right away. I think it was at this time that I found out the contents of Irvin's letter, which he had sent to Ron. He told Ron that he thought I would become a good missionary, but that he thought I needed to get married first, which, actually, was the philosophy of the DFM at the time. Nevertheless, Ron asked for time to consult with his colleagues before making a final decision, and I left with high hopes that I might become a missionary earlier than I expected.

It was not to be. About two months later, I received a letter from him stating that they were interested in my becoming a missionary, but they agreed with Irvin that I should get married first. This was rather frustrating, to say the least, as I did not want to be single either, but none of my dating efforts at AGTS had turned out well. Another frustrating part was that I was already showing signs of becoming a control freak, although I would not become aware of this trait for many years. I could control whether or not I met the other qualifications, like sufficient education, etc., but I could not help this one. While I did not mind graduating from CBC as a single, I had really hoped to meet someone at AGTS, but it just did not happen.

I got Ron's letter in about December, 1986, about six months before graduation. As I thought about ministry following AGTS, I tried to land a couple of positions on pastoral staffs, knowing that the DFM would I prefer that I had pastoral experience. But the Lord turned my heart to full time evangelism, which I had not expected to do beyond AGTS. As the calendar turned towards graduation, I increasing turned my attention to contacting pastors, for not only weekends, but also for four-night revival meetings that were normal in that time. I would move toward becoming a full-time evangelist.

Before I knew it, June 1987 had rolled around, and with it came graduation. My parents and Steve and Terrie all came to celebrate with me. The mind stretching hours over books and class assignments were coming to an end. Again, I had grown and matured, and it was time to say goodbye to the classmates and professors that I had come to love. Even back then, I sensed that my formal education was not yet finished, and that I would eventually go on for a doctorate. However, I knew that some time would pass before that would happen. With graduation came the normal uncertainties of what the future held, especially as to how and when I would become a missionary, but I was also excited about engaging the evangelistic ministry to which God was leading me to continue.

CHAPTER 7

Early Ministry Years

By the time I had graduated from AGTS, I had been traveling as an evangelist on the weekends for nearly three years. Most of my speaking engagements had been only on Sundays, but I had taken a few invitations to preach revival services lasting three or four nights. By this time, I had built up a good base of contacts, mostly within a four-hour radius of Springfield. But I also had scattered contacts elsewhere, including Michigan, because I had preached in some churches there while visiting home. However, my list of contacts was not enough at this point to move my ministry base there, or so I thought.

My plan was to keep the house in Springfield for when I was doing ministry there. I would also make trips to Michigan to start building a better base there, and possibility move back there in the future. I knew I could stay with my parents when ministering there. I also started working on making contacts with pastors in neighboring states like Illinois, Indiana and Ohio. Since Tim had graduated at the same time I did, keeping the house meant getting another roommate. I did, and it worked well for a couple of months. My new roommate, however, moved in without seeing the house first. After two months, he informed me that he needed a place with a larger kitchen. He abruptly left with no advance notice. Since no other roommate was immediately available, and I could not afford to pay the entire rent myself, I had no choice but to give up the house and move to Michigan.

I moved in December, 1987. My parents decided that I could live with them for up to six months. That would give me time to get settled and look for an apartment, and probably a roommate. Somehow, I found a place to stash all my stuff, taking over two of the upstairs bedrooms—one for my office. This was the very bedroom where I started praying for missionaries as a child. My six months with my parents would become six years.

The main reason that we got along so well was that they enjoyed having me home. Economics were another reason. It took time to build up enough meetings to be financially sustainable. Money was never my focus, but I did have to pay bills. Since my G.I. benefits ran out in the second year in AGTS, I ended up with just under $8,000 in school loans. While this was certainly a reasonable amount for seven years of education, it still meant making monthly payments on a small salary. Also, in 1989, my faithful Plymouth Volare that I had purchased back in 1978 had blown a cylinder and had to be replaced, which meant going into debt for a car.

I did augment my income by working a temporary job for a few weeks, but ultimately, this did not work out well because my availability was erratic. I was available some weeks but not others. God did, however, open other doors. While in school, I knew that writing would be a part of my ministry. As a result, I pursued and received an opportunity to write Sunday School lessons for the AG national Sunday School department. While the pay was not great, nor did I always have assignments, it did help. Best of all, it opened another avenue of ministry for me.

But God also opened another door, at least for one semester. A small independent Pentecostal Bible school had recently opened in Grand Rapids, and that they hired local ministers to teach on an as-needed basis. I contacted the school and got hired on to teach a course on the Life of Christ. My biggest challenge was that this meant that I had to be sure to be back in Grand Rapids every Thursday, but I made it work. Again, the pay was not great, but it helped. One of my students later became an AG pastor, and another became an AG missionary to Eastern Europe.

Running an evangelistic ministry was a full-time job. I would like to be able to say that I was able to spend the bulk of my time in prayer and study, but that was not the reality. While I certainly tried to do my best to make time for those things, calling pastors and doing the bookwork took up an enormous amount of time. I normally had to call a pastor four or five times just to get him on the phone. I had to learn to take "No" for an answer when pastors declined to schedule me for a meeting. One evangelist once gave me some wise words when he said that when pastors say, "No," it usually does not mean never, it just means no for that point in time. I think that most pastors that turned me down eventually invited me.

Cancellations were an occupational hazard and happened regularly. If a pastor gave me enough advance notice, it was normally not a problem to reschedule the date in another church. Most cancellations, however, came with only about six weeks or less notice and, those became harder to fill. Yet God somehow made a way, and as I became better established, I was able to fill those empty dates.

My greatest passion was to see people come to know Christ. My challenge was that most of the time I was preaching in churches where the people were already Christians! But I still faithfully gave altar calls, and a number of people came to know Christ every year. While the numbers were small, I know that God used me in people's lives. Fortunately, God opened some doors for me to get out of the churches and onto the streets.

While at AGTS, I became aware of the great need to share Christ, both the inner city and the suburbs. God began to plant a burden in my heart to reach the urban masses for Christ. I walked out part of this vision by focusing my ministry wherever possible in urban churches, both in the inner city and the suburbs.

In the summer of 1988, I signed up to participate in an urban outreach in Chicago which was sponsored by the youth department of the Illinois District of the Assemblies of God. When they found out that I was an evangelist, they graciously considered me one of the "ministry guests," and I was not required to pay anything to participate like the others had to do. We stayed on the campus of a local seminary and worked with churches in door-to-door evangelism. We held street meetings where we sang and preached. It was an incredible week. Then the something totally unexpected happened.

Afterward, while I was basking in the warm glow of a wonderful week of ministry, which included making a host of new friends, God spoke to me to take the same ministry concept back to Michigan to the city of Detroit. I was certain that he had dialed the wrong number. Credibility in ministry is based on relationships and a proven track record of ministry. At that point I did not have much of either. I had only been a member of the district for a few months at that time, and I am not certain that the district leadership even knew who I was. While I was greatly concerned about this, apparently the Holy Spirit was not, and my burden grew until I had to act.

The credibility that I did have stemmed at least partly from the fact that I came from one of the largest and most respected churches in the district, Grand Rapids First Assembly of God. Also, my pastor, Wayne Benson (who as a pastor and later friend probably had a greater impact on me than any other pastor), endorsed my ministry. When I called the district youth director, Steve Bach, to set up a meeting I could at least refer him to Wayne's endorsement. Steve did invite me for a meeting in September, 1988. The home missions' director, Dave Pace, also joined the meeting. At the meeting, they expressed interest in the idea, but Steve was not sure if the youth pastors in the district would be interested. He said that may have already laid their places for the following summer. He promised to contact some of the youth pastors and let me know.

The next few weeks were pure agony for me. I felt like I was "pregnant" with vision. After about six weeks, Steve called and said there were some guys that wanted to do it the following summer! Then he wanted to know when we could meet with all interested parties. This was the one and only time that a leadership meeting of what would come to be known as Detroit Outreach met according to my calendar!

There must have been about fifteen to twenty of us that gathered a month or so later. After opening the meeting Steve gave me the floor to share my vision. I came equipped with a map of the metro Detroit area, on which I had marked out the location of the AG churches, most of which I had not yet even visited. I explained that what we had done in Chicago was to send young people to do evangelism in connection with the local churches. One man who was there, Art Ledlie, who has invested his life in reaching Detroit for Christ, and would later become the director of the outreach, shared some thoughts that refined my ideas. And the plan was adopted. Once I had lit the match, Steve and Art took over and put the outreach together. That was fine with me because I wanted the district to take the leadership anyway. My role was to promote it as I traveled.

The next summer, we housed the participants in a gym owned by the church where Art was on staff. I was amazed and blessed beyond measure when I walked into that gym and saw 110 young people ready to hit the streets and share the love of Jesus Christ. They were the flesh and blood of the vision God had given me. Detroit Outreach became an annual event for seventeen years. Hundreds of young people participated. An untold number of people came to know Christ over the years, and some new churches were planted or strengthened by the Outreach.

One example remains fixed in my mind. One year, the district wanted to plant a church in Highland Park, one of the roughest areas of Detroit. To house the church, they bought a bankrupt movie theatre that specialized in pornographic films. I personally held the ladder while someone changed the movie marquee to announce the church that would be starting. I also remember cleaning at least one liquor bottle out of the men's bathroom. That church became a beacon of light to that community, leading many to Christ—many from some rough backgrounds.

Beginning in 1989, I began traveling back to the Philippines twice a year for evangelistic ministry. The door to full-time missions remained closed, but they welcomed me to come part-time. I continued doing the work of an evangelist there. Because I had no office help to keep the ministry running back home, I only went for three weeks at a time. It was the best I could do, and I loved every minute of it. After every trip, I filed a report of my ministry with the field director for DFM for the Asia Pacific region, Bob Houlihan. I had a feeling that sending in reports could be important for my future. Later, I would realize how right I was. Over the next three years, I made six trips.

By this time, I had discovered Psalm 2:8 (ESV) and claimed it as my life verse: "Ask of me, and I will make the nations your heritage, and the ends of the earth your possession." When I discovered this verse, I bought a map of the world and marked out the nations of Southeast Asia in a rectangle and hung it on the wall of my office. I was staking out the territory that God had laid on my heart. And yet, it seemed like it was not going to happen, as God just was not opening the door, at least to full-time service. I went through a period of time that I can only describe as "the valley of the death" of the vision as far as becoming a full-time missionary was concerned. I had to be content with going a couple of times a year while pursuing evangelistic work in the States. I actually began to doubt my missionary calling. I had to let the dream die and be content with what I had.

I made a lot of friends over those years, most of whom were pastors. I remain in contact with many of them to this day. Not long after I moved back to Michigan, I met a fellow evangelist named Phil Farnsworth, who became one of my closest friends. He was a computer whiz, and I ended up hiring him to do my newsletter databases, as well as my taxes. Even though we lived a couple of hours apart we saw each other often, or talked on the phone. We remained in close contact long after I went to the mission field until he went to be with the Lord. Such friendships have meant a great deal to me over the years.

Another close friend during that time was a man named John Haan. John and I had actually played baseball in the same Little League when we were kids, and we got reacquainted through my home church. John had married and had a family. He was working a secular job, but he was beginning to feel a call to the ministry. I brought him on board as a volunteer member of my team. We spent a lot of time together, and he traveled with me whenever I was speaking in the West Michigan area. In turn, he helped me with my newsletters and other things. It was a wonderful relationship. When he left the team to pastor a church, we remained in close contact for many years.

I also enjoyed being a part of the larger Assemblies of God fellowship. I attended as many sectional and district events as I could. There were three bi-annual general councils during these times. General councils were national gatherings of Assemblies of God ministers from all over America. A lot of these folks had the same challenges I did, and just being with them was encouraging to me. The same was true of the national Assemblies of God Evangelists' Fellowship to which I belonged. It was exciting to be a part of, and hopefully contribute to, a wider church family.

In 1991, God finally began to move me in the direction of foreign missions. I contacted Bob Houlihan, the field director to whom I had send all the reports of my short-term ministry. But instead of asking if I might go full-time, I inquired about becoming what was then called a missionary-evangelist, who spent half their time on the field and the other half at home raising funds for projects. I wanted to stay involved in such things like Detroit Outreach if I could, but I also had another that I did not share with Bob. I was absolutely paranoid about going to the field as a single man. I had learned to accept my singleness in America. Plus, I knew the language and the culture. Looking at it now, I see how contradictory my feelings were, knowing that God had called me, but being so afraid at the same time.

While waiting for Bob's response, I complained to another friend who had been travelling with me, that I had an open week in my schedule that I could not fill. I will never forget his response. He said something like, "You know, Dave, maybe there is going to be something that you are going to need to spend time praying about." I do not think he had any idea how prophetic he was. When I got home to Grand Rapids that same night, Bob Houlihan's reply was in a stack of mail that was waiting for me. He said he would be glad to have me apply to be a missionary, but that the missionary-evangelist category was closed, and I would have to live on the field full-time—the very thing I feared. Indeed, I needed to pray because I knew the direction in which the Spirit was pulling me. By the end of that week, I had faced my fear and God had given me peace about going to the field as a single man. This fear was never an issue again.

The next step was filling out a ton of paperwork, and taking a lot of physical and psychological tests, along with doing a couple of interviews. Finally, in May 1992, I was approved. The next step was a trip to Springfield for five weeks of training and commissioning. The first three weeks were spent reviewing mission policies and procedures, bonding with other missionary candidates, and doing whatever was necessary to prepare for our calling. Then, we were joined by veteran missionaries that were home itinerating that year. We had nine days of meetings within our region, as well as general meetings for inspiration. The last night was a commissioning service during which the leadership laid hands on us in prayer. We were then released to share the vision with churches and individuals, and raise the funds required to get to the countries of our calling.

For seven and-a-half years I had traveled as an evangelist, part-time at first and then full-time for five years. I had also found my calling. If I had gone to the field straight out of seminary, I would have gone without really knowing my place in the body of Christ. Now, I was sure of my calling as an evangelist. I had made a promise to God that if he ever called me to be an evangelist, I would focus on the preaching of the Word. To the best of my ability, I had kept that promise. In that sense, the negative experience that I had with an evangelist's ministry during my CBC days had been turned into something positive. I had matured, and by the grace of God, was ready for the next step.

In many respects, itineration was not much different than being an evangelist. I still had to make a ton of phone calls to pastors to set up services or appointments. I still had to travel. In fact, I had to travel more. I traveled more because instead of visiting one, or maybe two, churches a week, I was now visiting three; one on Sunday morning, another on Sunday night and another on Wednesday evenings. Occasionally, I found churches with Tuesday or Thursday night services. Since I had always preached missions in churches, even some of my preaching remained the same.

But there were a couple of major differences. One, my salary was now set and paid by the mission, so I was not directly dependent on offerings. I was no longer personally impacted by cancellations, although I still had to raise the funds to cover my salary and travel costs. Actually, while others took a pay cut to become missionaries, I got a raise! Second, I had to raise the funds to get to the field. There were two aspects to my budget. One, I had to raise $25,000 in cash for start-up funds. This went to pay for things like shipping my household goods to the field, and a myriad of other issues. Then, I had to raise nearly $5,000 a month in pledges that would sustain me once I reached the field. This would pay for things like language school and evangelistic outreaches, travel within Asia, my salary, health insurance, pension and a multitude of other expenses.

The original deadline was eighteen months, but I arrived at this deadline about $1,000 a month short in monthly pledges. I asked for, and received, a three-month extension. Fortunately, the district leaders were making an annual tour of the state, speaking in sectional meetings all over the state. They invited itinerating missionaries to attend the meetings, and briefly present their ministries to the pastors. Since I was the next missionary scheduled to leave, the district superintendent really pushed pastors to pledge to my ministry, and they responded favorably. That, along with other miracles, was enough to push me over my goal before the extension period expired.

Finally, the day came to leave, April 5, 1994. Two days earlier I had celebrated my 37th birthday on Easter Sunday. A couple of weeks before that my parents had given me a farewell party. I had also packed and shipped my personal belongings to Manila in a twenty-foot container. My mom, whose emotional battles had continued through the years, had to be hospitalized due to her trauma over my departure, despite the fact that she wholeheartedly endorsed my going. My dad had to get permission to take her out of the hospital to see me off at the airport. Other family members and friends also came. We cried and prayed together. As excited as I was to be on my way to fulfill God's call on my life, it was hard to say goodbye. But I understood that following Jesus has a price. Was I ultimately willing to pay it?

CHAPTER 8

The Early Years in the Philippines

I arrived in the Philippines about twenty-four hours after I had departed Grand Rapids. AG missionaries Herb and Karen Johnson (no relation) picked me up at the airport. Herb was the chairman of the Assemblies of God Missionary Fellowship (AGMF) in the Philippines at the time. They took me immediately to the home of Andy and Tess Jimenez and their children, A.J. and Yanyan, where I would live for over three years. They were a Filipino family and I had stayed with them on one of my short-term trips, so they already knew me, which was a key factor in my invitation to live with them. My friend Dwight Palmquist, the one who had invited me to the Philippines eleven years earlier, also lived there whenever he was in Manila. My request to stay with the Jimenezes was intentional. Beyond the obvious advantages of not having to rent my own place and cook my own food, etc., I wanted to be in a place where I could focus on learning Tagalog, the national language and Filipino culture by being totally immersed in it. Except for the fact that Andy and Tess preferred to speak to me in English, the setting was ideal.

I had to wait three weeks before beginning language study because no seat was available when I first arrived. I had written ahead to Herb to see if he would be willing to schedule me for some ministry, as I wanted to get started immediately. I had waited all these years to become a missionary and I did not want to waste a day. Herb was really helpful. I actually preached my first sermon within twelve hours of my arrival.

When I arrived, there was an invitation for me to speak at a Bible study at the offices of the International Correspondence Institute (ICI), now known as Global University in the United States. I had no time to prepare, but I went anyway. Herb also had some other engagements lined up for me, including speaking at the Chinese church in Manila where he and Karen were pastoring. I also accompanied a medical outreach team to the Northeastern part of Luzon, the main island. Then I went to the island of Leyte in the central eastern part of the country to participate in another type of outreach.

Finally, it was time to begin language study. I set the goal that I would not leave the language school until I could preach in Tagalog! I quickly learned that language study was like nothing I had ever done before in all my years of education. The closest anything had ever come were Greek and Hebrew studies at CBC and AGTS, but I never had to speak those languages. I only had to read them and translate them into English. Learning to read, write and speak a new language required developing an entirely new skill set, and it took all of my time and energy. Daily, I spent two hours in class, two hours practicing outside, and about two hours in study every night. It might not sound like a full load, but it really was. It was especially challenging—when just getting used to life in the Philippines, including the heat and humidity in Manila—also drained my physical and emotional resources. I am sure glad my leadership would not let me do much ministry during that time.

Determined to succeed, I went the extra mile and hired a language helper, in addition to attending classes. His name was Fred. In the beginning, he helped me review my lessons, as well as just giving me someone with whom to practice Tagalog. After a few weeks, I met a pastor who wanted to help me learn the language. He said if I would come to his church, he would give me five minutes every Sunday morning to share a testimony. I could say whatever I wanted as long as it was in Tagalog. This was a great opportunity, to not only practice the language, but to deal with "preacher's itch," since I was not allowed to preach during this time. Once I started doing this, Fred's main job was to help me prepare my testimonies, which I wrote out. Fred checked my grammar and marked the words for the appropriate pronunciation.

Being new to the language, mistakes were common—and some were really funny. One day, I was driving down a toll road north of Manila and had a car full of Filipinos. When we exited, I gave the lady in the toll booth too much money, which she immediately brought to my attention. I wanted to commend her, saying she was *matapat* (honest). Instead I told her she was *mataba* (fat)! As soon as the words were out of my mouth, I knew what I had said and was really embarrassed. Everybody else, including the lady herself, burst out laughing. The irony is that it was true. She was really fat! Fortunately, back then, it was taken as a compliment because Filipinos thought if you were fat, it meant that you had enough money to eat well.

Another funny situation happened a couple of years later when I was preaching in a church of about 250 people. Before my message, I was making some comments about the pastor's wife. However, I pluralized the word wife, making it sound like he had more than one! We all had a good laugh at my expense, and the pastor's wife did not seem to mind. The Bible teaches that "a merry heart does good like a medicine" (Proverbs 17:22). A good sense of humor is critical to adjusting to a new language and culture.

After a couple of months in language school, I decided it was time to pick up the pace. I went to the head teacher, Nenette Cada, who has since become a dear friend. I asked her if I could add one session a week, and she reluctantly agreed. After all, with people dying and going to Hell, I wanted to get busy reaching them! This was an act of faith for Nenette because, in truth, I was not doing all that well in grasping the language. But she could see that I was really working hard at it, and decided to give me the benefit of the doubt. Many months would pass before she would see the reward of her labors.

After about four months of study, I took a break to attend some Assemblies of God World Missions' meetings in Seoul, Korea. One of them was the first gathering of the World Assemblies of God Fellowship. We had an amazing couple of days meeting at the famed Yoido Full Gospel Church pastored by David Yonggi Cho. I think the church had over 500,000 members even back then. I really saw the power of prayer, and my prayer life was forever changed. For many years, I had devotions in whatever part of the day I had time. After that, I moved my devotions to first thing in the morning, and they have been much more consistent, enriching and rewarding.

My slow progress in the Tagalog language continued until about the end of my seventh month in the program. While my teachers despaired a bit, as did I, over my struggles to learn the language, neither they nor I gave up. Finally, it began to pay off. Somehow, the synapses in that linguistic part of my brain began to snap in place. From that point on, my improvement in Tagalog became meteoric, and as part of the final part of the program, I preached my first sermon in Tagalog.

The message was drawn from Jesus and the Samaritan woman in John 4. It took me at least three months to prepare it. The content was not the problem. I determined from the beginning that I would write the message in Tagalog, not English. One of my missionary friends wrote his messages in English, had them translated, and then preached in Tagalog, but I wanted to use Tagalog from the beginning. Fred and I spent many hours working through the text of the message. Finally, the day came. I was invited to speak in a Wednesday night service at the church I was attending. Nenette and one of the other teachers came to grade my performance because it was, after all, part of my language studies. Everything was scripted from my opening prayer, to the message and the altar call. It lasted about forty-five minutes. I felt bad for my listeners! Nenette was among those who responded to the altar call. In the process, something changed the event for her from a school assignment into real ministry. I am glad someone was touched that night, and I achieved my goal of not leaving language school until I could preach in the language.

Preaching in Tagalog at this point did not mean I did it with great proficiency. I continued to write out my entire sermon each time I preached and I read my sermon from the manuscript. It took about a year and-a-half for me to break free of the manuscripts, but I eventually preached with only typical sermon notes. I eventually became proficient enough to preach without any notes in front of me at all.

About a week after finishing language school I celebrated my 38th birthday and my first-year anniversary on the field. I decided to celebrate in style with a lot of friends. Tess agreed to host the party at our house, but disagreed when I only wanted to serve cake and ice cream—a typical American party. She said her reputation as a hostess was at stake, and that if I wanted a party, it had to be a full dinner. I agreed, and spent $300 on a great evening with about forty friends. I also learned a valuable lesson about shame and honor in the Philippines. I was glad that Tess spoke up.

I was ready to hit the road. By this time, I had been given a Nissan Pathfinder truck, provided by the Speed-the-Light (STL) program of the Assemblies of God young people in the United States--specifically, those in my home state, Michigan. The same program had also provided me with a sound system for our evangelistic outreaches. We were also given generous grants by the AG's men's literature ministry, Light for the Lost (LFTL). Although I do not have the financial totals available, it is likely that LFTL has invested at least $100,000 in our ministry over the years. The AG children's program, the Boys and Girls Missionary Challenge (BGMC) also played a role in resourcing some of our literature needs.

I hired Fred, my language helper, to be my first ministry assistant. We took off for other parts of the country in response to invitations from a number of district superintendents. We would normally spend about three weeks in each region. We followed a schedule set for us by the superintendents, spending two to three nights in each place. Later, we came to the conclusion that three nights in each placed worked best for us, and we stuck with that schedule for years. As I gained experience in leading this ministry, we eventually developed a team manual of best practices, which were learned through lessons from others, as well as trial and error. We then worked with each pastor to follow the manual everywhere we went. By and large, this worked well.

Like Dwight Palmquist had done with me years earlier, I invited a young college intern named John Vincen from the States to travel with us over his summer vacation. We went to the central part of the Philippines to an island called Panay and to a couple of smaller islands in the area. John would prove to be a great asset to the work. Later, John became a missionary to Indonesia and has now been there for several years.

At one point, I took a special class at the Asia Pacific Theological Seminary (APTS). I had observed that many, if not most, Filipinos followed a more popular brand of Catholicism known as "folk Catholicism" or "animistic Catholicism." Animism is the belief that the world is full of spirits that can be manipulated, or appeased, to do what people need or want. Witchcraft, sorcery, divination, rites, rituals, amulets and talismans are the means to that end. This course would whet my interest for what would become a lifelong research interest, which would ultimately go beyond the Philippines. That interest brought me to the point that I now teach that class at APTS.

In November, 1995, I got a call from my dad that my mother had become seriously ill. She had problems in her intestines, and she would probably die. Dad asked me to come home. I was shocked. I had no idea that she was even sick. Since they did not know what was going to happen, I could not make a decision on where I would go, so I had to wait. Two days later, Dad called back to say Mom had been air-medevacked to the Mayo Clinic in Rochester, Minnesota, one of the best hospitals in the world. I jumped on the first plane available. It was one of the longest trips of my life, not knowing if my mother would be dead or alive by the time I got there. I met a Methodist preacher on the same plane and he comforted me with his presence. We stopped in Seattle and I was able to get word that Mom was still with us.

When I arrived in Rochester, my younger brother, Tom, and his wife picked me up. They said there were all kinds of tubes attached to mom's body. She looked terrible. Then he added, "Dave, here's the deal. We keep a smile on our faces when we're with Mom. Then we go out in the hallway and cry on each other's shoulders." We would do a lot of that over the next few weeks. Mom was awake and alert when I arrived and recognized me instantly. It was a nice ending to a long journey.

Tom was still in the Navy and he was stationed at a naval base north of Chicago at the time. He had to return to his duties after the first weekend I was there. Also, my older brother, Steve, had a job that kept him in Grand Rapids most of the time. So, Dad and I were Mom's main companions. For the next several weeks, we were at the hospital all day and sometimes into the evening. We played cards in the visitor's lounge when Mom was resting, and hung out in her room when she was able to have company. Steve brought his family for a weekend, and my two nephews and niece brightened our days.

At one point, Mom had surgery to remove part of her intestines. She was in the operating room for eleven hours, far longer than the doctors originally projected. By the time it was over, Dad and I were beside ourselves with worry, even though someone from the operating room updated us by phone every couple of hours. When we saw Mom, her face was bloated almost beyond recognition because of the fluids they had pumped into her body during the surgery. It was only temporary, but Dad later said he wished we had not gone to see Mom after the surgery. But human nature being what it is, we would have wanted to see her, and most likely would have done so, even if we had known what a shock her appearance would be.

While we were there, my maternal grandmother—that is, my mom's mother, went to be with the Lord at the age of 83. We had a chaplain at Mayo help us break the news to Mom, but it was still hard.

At one point, I complained to Dad that I felt worthless because I was not accomplishing work while I was there, although I was invited to speak at a Wednesday night service in a local AG church during their missions' convention. Dad immediately rebuked me, saying that just my being there for him and Mom was important to them. It was a good lesson that "being" was more important than "doing." Given my tendency to be extremely goal oriented, it was not a lesson that I have learned easily, and I have had to be reminded often. But I was glad to be there for both of them.

After three to four weeks, it became obvious that Mom was going to recover and we were all rejoicing in the Lord. Before going back to the Philippines, I flew to Grand Rapids for a week and spent Thanksgiving with Steve and his family. I also went to see my mom's brother and sister and comforted them in the passing of their mother and my grandmother. My uncle was slowly dying of cancer, and it would be the last time I would ever see him on earth. He passed away at the age of 52 about nine months later. He and my grandmother were both believers and I know I will see them again someday. The hope of heaven does make grief easier to bear, but there was still a lot of grief and emotional trauma all in the same time period. When I first went to the field, I had to cope with the reality that I might not be there when my loved ones died, but it is all part of the price of following God's call. It was really hard, but God was faithful. We also had many friends and relatives that walked with us through this time.

When I returned to the Philippines, an invitation to China was waiting for me. An old friend from AGTS, who was serving as a missionary to China, invited me to come and speak at a missionary retreat the following February, 1996. I readily accepted and had a great time ministering to those who really needed the fellowship and appreciated the ministry of the Word. I think that the situation in China did not give them much opportunity for fellowship with other believers, so they all seemed to enjoy the event.

Around the same time, I also made a trip to Taiwan at the invitation of a missionary named Dick Adams. I had met Dick in the Philippines, when at the request of the field leadership, I hosted him for an evangelistic outreach in Metro Manila while I was going to language school. Dick and another missionary couple, Mike and Jane Ann McAteer, had a strong ministry to Filipino overseas workers who were living in Taiwan. They asked me to come during the Chinese New Year, a week when most of the Filipinos would be off from their regular jobs. I spent a few days with Dick in Taipei before going to Taichung on the western side of the island. I spoke mainly at special events. If only Filipinos and missionaries were present, I spoke in Tagalog. The last Sunday I was there I spoke in the international church that Dick, along with his wife, Pat, pastored in Taipei. I have remained in contact with Mike, and to a lesser extent, Dick, ever since.

Sometime in 1996, God began to give me a burden for teenagers. I sensed that many were lost and searching for truth. Fred and I conceived the idea of speaking in high schools as we traveled doing our evangelistic rallies; it was a good, natural fit. We found a nationwide moral recovery group that was holding rallies in high schools. We joined the group to gain access to the schools. We asked the churches that invited us to do outreaches for them to include high schools. While the response was a bit lukewarm, and I did not have the leadership skills or influence that I would later have, they were open. They helped set up and do the rallies. I spoke, and we passed out tons of gospel literature provided by the AG men's Light for the Lost program right on the school grounds. But my lack of leadership skills and influence at the time meant that agreeing to participate in a high school rally did not necessarily mean being able to do the follow-up. I had to be content with seeing it as a seed sowing ministry. After all, if one wants to reap an abundant harvest, one must sow seed abundantly as well. Over the course of a couple of years, we visited approximately eighty-five high schools and spoke to tens of thousands of students. This ministry came to an end with the conclusion of our first term. Then, we moved to an area where another ministry was impacting high schools, and we did not wish to interfere with them, nor were we given the opportunity to participate with them.

That year we also started ministering to the children that were attending our evangelistic rallies. The method was quite simple. We did a thirty-minute program with singing geared to their age. Then we told a story that contained biblical truth. Finally, we gave an altar call just for them. We also passed out Christian literature in comic book form in the Tagalog language. We learned that each comic book in the Philippines was read by around fifty-three people, so we knew that these comics would also find their way into the hands of adults as well. At this point, ministry to children in the churches was not as well-developed as it is today. But at the time, we had to be content, again, simply sowing the seed into the hearts of the children. Also, we demonstrated to the churches both the need of, and value in, ministering to these precious ones.

In May of 1996, Fred and I loaded my STL vehicle onto a car ferry and set off for the island of Palawan. Here Fred's time with the ministry came to an unanticipated end due to personal problems. Fred had been a friend, ministry assistant and great language helper, and I was sad to see him go. Fortunately, my proficiency in Tagalog had improved to the point that I no longer needed as much help as I had in the past, but I would miss him. After the tour, the district superintendent accompanied me to Manila so I would not have to travel alone, which is not a good idea for an American. Even though I spoke the language, there were still many ways in which I could have been taken advantage of, and having a Filipino with me mitigated those possibilities.

My next ministry tour was in Bicol, which comprises the southern third of the island of Luzon that I had first visited in 1983. Jesse Tan, (the man who had pioneered the church in Tabaco that I had assisted in planting) had become the district superintendent. I knew that he would have ministry assistants available to help, so I decided to make the 12-hour drive alone. This was not a smart move, but no one was available to accompany me. I went fully loaded with all of my equipment, literature and personal baggage. All went well—except for not one, but two—flat tires along the way. One tire had a total blowout, which required purchasing a new tire. Fortunately, I knew a local pastor near where it happened, and he took me to a reputable place where I bought a good, new tire. I eventually made it to the Tan's home about 10 p.m. After that, I seldom made long trips alone again.

Pedio Belaro, a member of Jesse's church, who had accompanied Fred and me on a previous tour, joined the team for this tour as well. But Jesse also had another member, Alan Esplana, a single man in his early twenties, that also accompanied us. We had a great time together, traveling the region and seeing people saved and healed. I bonded well with Pedio and Alan. Jesse had already been a good friend for some time. I wanted to take Pedio as my new full-time assistant, but Jesse wanted me to take Alan, as he needed Pedio at the church. I trusted Jesse's judgment and invited Alan to join me, and he accepted. It was one of the best decisions I ever made.

I had always wanted to do a doctorate in missiology, which is the study of missions. It involves academic disciplines like theology and anthropology, as well as other behavioral science disciplines in combination with each other. I felt like I needed at least one term of missionary experience before I began to work on a doctorate. As I completed my second year on the field, I wanted to start looking at doctoral programs, and perhaps see where I would like to do my studies when the time came.

One night, I had dinner with Melvin and Louise Ho, who were serving as AGWM missionaries at APTS. Melvin and I had been classmates at AGTS several years before. Melvin was working on his doctorate at the time, and so I decided to ask for his advice on how to proceed. He encouraged me to write a master's thesis first, in preparation for doctoral studies. He explained that doing a thesis would help me gain the critical thinking and writing skills that I would need to do a doctorate well. The more I prayed about it, the more I believed that this was God's guidance to me. The direction the Holy Spirit led me would impact my life in ways I could have never imagined.

I consulted with John Carter, another AGWM missionary, who was serving as the president of APTS. He said that I could do a thesis without doing another degree, but that I would have to take a special course in advanced theological research methods. He was planning to teach that course during the September-December trimester in 1996. He explained that I would need to be on campus three days a week, leaving me the rest of the week for evangelistic outreaches. After more prayer, I decided to take the course.

As it turned out, I was the only student in John's class. While it was common to cancel classes with such a low turnout, John opted not to do so, and I was glad he did. I spent the next three months studying various research methodologies, including statistical analysis. I also was preparing my research proposal for approval, all the while carrying on my evangelistic ministry three days a week. Most of our meetings were about three hours' drive from Baguio, so I commuted back and forth, leaving Alan with the equipment and the pastors.

One day, while going to the library, I noticed a lady, whom I assumed was an American, sitting and talking with someone just outside the library. Since she was talking with someone, I did not stop to introduce myself as I would have ordinarily done. Since I knew most of the faculty and because APTS usually has one or two Americans studying there at any given time, I just assumed that she was some student's wife. A few days later I passed by the campus postal boxes and saw a box labelled, "Debbie Langley Visiting Faculty." Then the lights went on in my brain, and I figured that it was her I had seen on the way to the library.

Since the sign did not indicate that she was married, I went into "bachelor mode" and determined that I needed to check her out. Doing so would lead to another life-changing experience.

CHAPTER 9

Debbie

I decided to look for her in chapel since everyone was expected to gather there three times a week. I found her, and the two seats next to her were open, so I proceeded to occupy one of them. After the service, she introduced herself and we chatted briefly before going our separate ways. A few days later, I saw her at a birthday party in a crowded apartment. I sat right next to her so I could talk with her, knowing full well that tongues would wag. Later, she admitted that she was embarrassed, but I was not. I was a man on a mission.

About that time, APTS celebrated its annual "International Night," when all of the students and faculty cook food from their homelands to share, dress in their national costumes, and have lots of skits and songs. I was suffering from conjunctivitis, or "pink eye," in both eyes at the time. I saw Debbie at the dinner and asked her if she would accompany me to town to buy medicines later. I told her I would buy her ice cream at McDonalds. She agreed to go with this 6'5" pink-eyed giant and we had a good time.

On campus, I stayed with a missionary widow named Leota Morar, who was old enough to be my mother, and her housekeeper. Debbie had heard that I was interested in participating in a small group which met on Fridays in lieu of chapel, and she needed help in leading her group. For some unknown reason, she was assigned to lead a small group alone, which was not standard practice. She approached Leota and asked if I would be interested in helping her. When Leota mentioned this to me, she said that she did not think Debbie had any ulterior motives. I remember thinking that I might not object if she did! I agreed, the only misgiving was that I would miss out on the cinnamon rolls that Leota always offered her group. When I showed up at Debbie's house, I told her I would stay only if the snacks she served were as good as Leota's. I got the answer I deserved when she coolly replied, "You can leave now!" I stayed.

I was glad I did because that is how we really got acquainted. Debbie had some young men in her group that really needed the guidance of an older brother, which was one of the reasons Debbie had invited me to help in the first place. I connected with them quite well. Also, I was having some problems in my evangelistic ministry, and Debbie was impressed that I was willing to share about them and ask for prayer. It was during these weeks that we began to fall in love with one another, and the Lord began to knit our hearts together. After a few weeks, I began taking her out on dates to downtown Baguio, which had a number of places that were conducive to romance and the relationship blossomed.

Neither one of us took dating lightly. We both understood that step had moved us to being more than just friends, and it would either lead to marriage or to broken hearts—which we hoped to avoid. In some respects, then, it was only a matter of time. Dating took on a new purpose, albeit one with lots of laughter and good times, including me singing love songs to her at the top of my lungs in downtown Baguio with lots of people within hearing range. This really embarrassed her—which was part of the fun. We began to talk seriously about marriage and share our dreams for the future. Both of us informed our families about the relationship and prayed for God's guidance. At this point, I was on the road about 250 nights a year doing evangelism. I asked Debbie if she could handle 200 nights a year on the road, knowing that if she could not do 200, there was no hope of doing 250. She said no. I went to prayer again. I said, "Lord, I don't need to know the future. I just need to know that marrying Debbie is your plan." Neither of us wanted to ruin the ministry because of marriage. God's answer was like the old Nike commercial "Just do it!" I had my answer.

The next step was to determine where and when I would propose. By this time, we were well into December, and Debbie had come home with me to Manila for the holidays. Tess made sure that Debbie was welcomed and well-chaperoned to avoid any hint of impropriety. She put Debbie in a guest room as far away from my room as possible! At that time, the missionary fellowship had an annual meeting for several days over New Year's, usually at some nice resort. This particular year we went to a beachside resort in Tacloban City on the island of Leyte. I decided that the beach would be a great place for a marriage proposal, and resolved to propose on New Year's Eve.

Once we arrived, I began checking out the lay of the land, unbeknownst to Debbie, to determine the best spot for the proposal. I left nothing to chance. I found a short beach retainer wall on the perimeter of the beach with the Leyte Gulf in the background. Perfect! When the time came, however, I did have to make one small adjustment. Somehow, the selected spot had gained a horrible fish smell and I had to move us down the wall about fifty feet, but the spot was still beautiful. I had her sit on the wall while I dropped to one knee. I looked straight at her and popped the question. She said, "Yes," and I was thrilled beyond words!

We decided that our engagement would not be official until I talked to Debbie's dad, so we did not tell too many people at the annual meeting, although I think some guessed it by the look on our faces. Because I was planning to spend the following week in Eastern Samar, with no way to call States, we decided to wait a week to call her folks. When we did, Debbie called first to make the case to her dad about our marriage, and then I called. I was really nervous, especially since I had never met the man. I will never forget his answer to my request for Debbie's hand in marriage. He said, "Dave, all of her life we have taught Debbie how to hear the voice of God, and if she has heard the voice of God regarding marrying you, that's good enough for us, and you have our blessings." Once again, I was stupendously pleased. But later we heard a rumor about another reason he might have had for saying yes. Debbie is the oldest child and has four brothers, all of whom were married by this time. The rumor was that Debbie's mom had a shotgun she would have used on Dad if he had he said, "No." She was not going to be denied becoming the mother of the bride! To this day, however, I must add that the rumor has never been confirmed, and no shotgun has ever been found. Afterwards, we talked to my parents, and following mission policy, got approval from AGWM. Then, we shouted the good news from the housetops.

I would have preferred to marry Debbie immediately. But weddings do take a bit of time to plan, and we had mission responsibilities that we wanted to fulfil first. Debbie was scheduled to teach a crash course in English for new students over the summer break, which is from late March to early June in the Philippines. I had to do field research for my masters' thesis. Therefore, we decided to wait until July. Over the ensuing months I constantly traveled between my home in Manila, Debbie in Baguio, and my field research in the Leyte/Samar region in the central eastern part of the Philippines. We also did evangelistic rallies as we went along. I was also getting us ready to live in a house on a Bible school campus in Pangasinan, about two hours south of Baguio. I did not spend much time in Manila during those months.

There were a couple of memorable events that happened during this time, one of them hilarious, and the other quite serious. One day, a district superintendent, Alejandro Langiden and I were planning our schedule for a series of meetings in his area for the month of February that year. We were discussing doing a meeting over Valentine's Day. Having not had anyone special in my life for years, I was not thinking about the significance of the day. Fortunately, Pastor Langiden was, and he suddenly asked me, "Don't you want to spend Valentine's Day with Debbie?" "O yeah," I replied, and thanked him for mentioning it. When

Debbie heard this, she decided she really liked this man. We celebrated Valentine's Day at Debbie's home in Baguio, and she made it a really memorable day with a homecooked meal in her backyard.

The other event was a great victory for Christ. We conducted an outreach in Villasis, Pangasinan, about a two-hour drive down the mountain from Baguio and not far from the AG Bible school where we were to live after the wedding. One night we showed a film called *Hinugot Sa Dalim* (Snatched from the Darkness), which tells the story of a young woman whom God delivers from the web of witchcraft. I often augmented the film by preaching from I Kings 18, where Elijah had a power encounter with the prophets of Baal. I drew a comparison to those practicing witchcraft in the Philippines. On this night, unbeknownst to me, there were a number of practicing witches in the crowd. Curiously enough, some of them had been sending their children to Sunday school at the AG church.

Some of the witches were understandably unhappy with the film and my message. They did not like the unfavorable comparison to the prophets of Baal. One of them really took issue with the pastor after my message. The following night, they turned out early to continue their debate with me. They were so upset that they called the village council to a special meeting held at the location of our rally. They hauled me in front of the council to demand an apology. When the village captain asked me to apologize, which I could not in good conscience do, I had a bit of a dilemma. To say, "No" directly in this situation would have been unnecessarily offensive in Filipino culture. It would have been seen as disrespectful to the village council, whose only desire was to maintain peace in the community.

So, I declined to apologize, but I spoke in an indirect manner. Since the witches had twisted my words into something that I did not actually say, I launched into a long explanation of what I had said, in effect re-preaching part of my message. In time, the village captain realized that I was not going to apologize, and he determined that the matter would have to be resolved in court. After the meeting broke up, one of the other leaders told me privately that the witches involved were his children, and he would make sure that the matter went no further. He kept that promise.

Later, much to my joy, I heard that some of the witches came to Christ. Unfortunately, others did not. I was told that one of those who did not accept Jesus became demon possessed, which was hardly a surprise. The others tried to drive out the demon by beating the person's head into the floor, accidentally killing him. The mayor's office was called in to investigate, but I never heard what the outcome was. Either way, this, and the fact that some of them got saved, probably put an end to this particular coven.

By about April, I was far enough along in my master's thesis to begin the field research. Alan, a summer intern named Leon Davis, and I headed for Leyte and Samar to do the research and some evangelism. We hired a team of researchers, and over the course of a couple of months we interviewed a total of seventy witchdoctors about their practices. My intent was to learn all I could about them, and then expose their practices to the light of God's word in my preaching, teaching and writing. I do not advocate that anyone should do this unless they have a word from God to do so, which I did, because these people are in contact with demonic spirits in rebellion against God. He did, indeed, protect me and my team that entire time. While we witnessed some Satanic rituals and practices, we were not adversely affected by them. The fruit from this research will be noted in a later chapter. It is sufficient to say here that my goal in learning, and exposing, the deeds of darkness to the truth of God's word has been abundantly achieved. Debbie participated through intercessory prayer from Baguio.

While I was doing my research, Debbie conducted an intense course in English for incoming APTS students. In the meantime, Debbie's mother and sisters-in-law were recruited to help with the wedding planning and execution. When Debbie completed the English course, she went home to Bellevue, Washington, which is just east of Seattle, about five weeks before the wedding. Her family had lined up all kinds of activities related to wedding preparations, including making Debbie's wedding dress with materials she brought home from Baguio. Debbie's mom even made sure that I, and all three of my groomsmen, were measured for tuxes.

I arrived and met Debbie's family just twelve days before the wedding. In those days, taking a razor on a plane was not a problem, so I made sure I was shaved and cleaned up to meet Debbie's folks at the airport! I was a bit nervous, and it did not help, when while waiting for my bags, Debbie's dad suddenly disappeared and no one knew where he went. He eventually resurfaced and all was well after that. We hit it off pretty well.

I was invited to preach at Debbie's home church the Sunday before the wedding. This gave her parents another opportunity to check me out a bit. Two days later, just four days before the wedding, my parents, my Aunt Kathie, and Steve and Terrie arrived, and I was given the task of showing them around the area. Other than that, my only job was to make sure the groomsmen got their tuxes and showed up for the wedding. Debbie's mom, along with the wedding planner from the church, had things well in hand.

Debbie's mother comes from a family of ten children, and most of Debbie's aunts and uncles—and even a few of her thirty-three cousins—were there, along with all four of her brothers, their families and lots of friends. Even a few of our fellow missionaries were able to come. Overall, there were about 250 people there. The wedding and reception, which was held in the church's fellowship hall, went off with only one hitch. Debbie's youngest brother and his wife had problems getting the candles lit right before the wedding procession was to enter the sanctuary.

After spending our wedding night in a hotel in Seattle, we went up to a hot springs resort in Harrison, British Columbia, where Debbie's parents had often vacationed, and which they strongly recommended.

We enjoyed ourselves immensely. After a few days there, we went to Leavenworth, Washington, a tourist town of German vintage. We had looked forward to strolling among the shops and restaurants and just having time together. However, I had come down with the flu toward the end of our stay in Harrison and spent most of the time in Leavenworth in bed, much to our dismay. Several years later we were able to return there for a night and were able to do at least some of the things that Debbie had wanted to do while we were on our honeymoon. These days came to an end far too quickly and we returned to Bellevue to begin married life. But there was one hiccup. I had to have hernia surgery, and the only time it fit in our schedule was right after our honeymoon.

Fortunately, it was outpatient surgery that went well. A week, or so later we headed for Grand Rapids. My family was waiting to host us for a post-wedding reception for my friends and family that could not attend the wedding. Like the wedding, this was well-attended, but our situation was then reversed. I knew everybody that came, and it was Debbie who was meeting new friends and relatives. As at the wedding, we all had a good time.

When people asked us if we preferred cash as a wedding gift, we responded in the affirmative. This allowed us to buy what we needed when we returned to the Philippines, and people responded well. As usual, some people preferred to give actual gifts, which was also fine with us. In cases where we received duplicate gifts, such as an iron, we simply brought one to the Philippines and stored the other in the States for when we were on furlough. Nothing had to be exchanged. We stored some things with Debbie's parents and some things with mine.

AGWM was kind enough to give us several weeks in the States for the wedding, honeymoon and everything else. By September, it was time to head back to the Philippines to complete my first term. We could have stayed home and begun itineration, since there were only about seven months left on my first term. But I felt it was important to complete the entire four years, and Debbie was agreeable to that plan.

As mentioned above, we rented a small house on a Bible college campus that was about two hours south of Baguio and four hours north of Manila. We took this opportunity because most houses in Manila were only rentable on a year-long contract, and we would not be there that long. The rent in Pangasinan was much more reasonable, and the money went to support an AG Bible school, so both we and the Bible school leadership were happy with the arrangement.

Having a house, however, did not necessarily mean that we were home much. Our original plan was to travel only half the time because we both knew that continual travel would be hard on Debbie. But since we had little other reason to sit at home, and many invitations to travel and preach the gospel, our plan went by the wayside. We spent more time on the road than we had originally planned. On the positive side, we got to hold a lot more meetings than we originally projected, and a lot more people heard the gospel. On the other hand, however, Debbie's health did suffer, and a doctor finally ordered her to stay home. Since we had made a commitment not to be separated in our first year of marriage, that meant staying home more, or at least, scheduling outreaches close enough to home to commute back and forth without staying overnight.

To this point, Debbie had invested most of her time at APTS, and had not been deeply immersed in Filipino language and culture. This radically changed once we started traveling together. At that time, we mainly stayed in people's homes as we traveled. On some occasions, the only thing that separated our bed from others was a mosquito net! The Philippines is still a developing nation, and we spent a lot of time in the rural areas, where life can be rather rough for westerners. I thought she took it all in stride, but later she told me that the first year of our marriage was tough on her. In truth, I was not always sensitive to her feelings.

In January of the following year, 1998, we were invited to Indonesia for ministry by AG missionaries Charlie and Nada Dates, who we had met at a missionary meeting in the Philippines the previous year. We went to a number of places in the Kalimantan Rain Forest on the

Indonesian part of the island of Borneo. We taught seminars and preached. In one situation, a young woman who had been cursed by a spiritist was wonderfully set free when we prayed for her. In one meeting a number of people fell to the floor under the power of the Spirit.

I will never forget the little village of Tumbang Kunyi, which is along a river among the Dayak people just south of the equator. We were there to teach some seminars for a fledgling AG church that two young ladies from a Bible school were planting there. While there, we had a couple of unforgettable experiences. First, one night, a mentally deranged murderer escaped from a local prison in the middle of the night. He woke up half the village, including Debbie, as well as Charlie and Nada. Meanwhile, I slumbered along peacefully at Debbie's side under a mosquito net in the middle of the living room floor. Since misery loves company, Debbie decided that I needed to be awake and worried too, so she woke me up. I somehow failed to appreciate the situation. Eventually things settled down and I was allowed to go back to sleep.

Many of the Dayaks are nominally Protestant but they also routinely practice spiritism. They had once been head-hunters. Any number of homes in the area had a spirit pole in front of the house, with a human skull buried beneath it to ward off evil spirits. One day, we taught a seminar in such a home. We could feel the presence of the forces of darkness when we passed by the pole. The resident, who was a Christian, explained that he wanted to remove the pole, but because the house was owned by his entire family, he did not want to do so until he had received their permission. Since the house belonged to all, this was the correct approach in this situation, and we commended him for it. The seminar I led that day dealt with a biblical perspective on spiritism. I do not know whether that pole was ever removed. I do know that the church that was planted became a beacon of light to the entire community, and they have planted three more churches in that area.

I continued work on my master's thesis, and I completed it shortly before we returned to the States for itineration in April 1998. Before we knew it, April arrived and with it, the completion of my first four-year term. For most missionaries, the first term is the hardest. More missionaries drop out during the first term than any other. By God's grace, we had survived, and for the most part, thrived.

Since most of our supporting churches were in the Midwest, there was not much discussion on whether we would live in Bellevue or Grand Rapids. We visited with Debbie's family for a week or two, as well as speaking in some churches in the area. Then, we loaded the wedding presents that we had left with Debbie's parents into a rental car and drove across the country. In nine days, we drove about 3,100 miles, preached in five churches, and visited two national parks. We passed through a part of the country neither of us had ever seen. It was an enjoyable trip, but we were exhausted by the time we arrived in Michigan.

After staying with my parents for a few weeks, we moved into a nice apartment complex about 15 minutes away, so we saw them often. This was a bit strange for me in the beginning, as this was the first time I had ever lived anywhere in Grand Rapids except my parents' home, and it took a bit of adjusting.

The year at home passed quickly, as we visited well over 100 churches in a number of states. We racked up around 50,000 miles of travel in that 12-month period. God was moving in a powerful season of revival in my home church, which Debbie had also joined. They were having special Friday night revival services, which we attended as much as we could. Revival was also happening in Pensacola, Florida, the Seattle area, and in the little town of Smithton, Missouri, at the time. We were able to work in trips to these places as well, and participated in what God was doing at the time.

As we prepared to return to the Philippines in about May 1999, Debbie felt the Lord impressing her to get a mammogram. We had already passed the physical exams required by AGWM to return to the field. For some strange reason they did not require women Debbie's age to get a mammogram, although that later changed. But since she felt God speaking to her to do it, we scheduled an appointment, and the mammogram came back positive. This called for a sonogram, which also came back positive. The next step was a biopsy, which involved outpatient surgery. Many people told us that the biopsy is usually benign, so we did not worry about it. We headed out for a previously scheduled vacation at a cabin in the woods of northern Georgia. By this time, we had moved out of our apartment, and we were staying with my folks temporarily before we left for the field.

While on vacation, we called the surgeon's office and received word that the biopsy result was not what we had hoped. Debbie had breast cancer. The doctor said that they caught it early, and that this was the best kind of cancer one could get, but it was still cancer! We were shocked, and temporarily devastated when they recommended another biopsy and six weeks of radiation. We were understandably stunned and grieved, but God was with us the whole way. Fortunately, the second biopsy revealed that there was no more cancer. All that remained to be done were thirty radiation treatments, which were done daily over about a six-week period. Then, we had to wait a couple of weeks for final clearance from the doctors.

Meanwhile, we were not idle. With permission from our leaders to stay in the States and continue as much itineration as we could, we continued visiting churches. We could not travel far because Debbie needed to go to the hospital five days a week for the treatments. At the beginning of this time period, we had no services scheduled because we expected to be back in the Philippines. Amazingly, God opened doors, and we filled every Sunday morning, Sunday night and Wednesday night for the entire additional time that we had to be home! Additionally, we were able to get about $11,000 from BGMC and other sources to fulfill a long-held dream of buying books for the Bible schools in the Philippines. Grand Rapids is home to several major Christian publishers, and most had an outlet for selling books, used and new, at discounted prices. We had a lot of fun browsing their bookshelves. and buying around 1,000 books, which we then packed and shipped to Manila before we left. More importantly, as things turned out, we had three additional months with my family, especially my parents. As we headed back to the Philippines around July 1999, little did we know that we would not see my mother again this side of heaven.

CHAPTER 10

Manila Again and the Move to Bicol

The first order of business upon our return to the Philippines was to send Debbie to language school, which meant locating in Manila for the first year of the new term. The school that Debbie attended was not the same as I had attended back in 1994-95. That school had closed, but the head teacher, Nenette Cada, had opened her own her own school, His Name Language Center, in Quezon City. Rather than get a house or apartment, we had made arrangements to live with the Jimenezes, the family that I had lived with before we were married. While it required that we had only two private rooms, one of which I used as a small office and a bathroom, which we had to share with another renter, it also had a number of advantages. It was close to the language school, meaning that we did not have to contend much with Manila's legendary traffic jams. Since Tess, the lady of the house, employed maids, Debbie had no domestic responsibilities. Living with Filipinos gave Debbie ready-made opportunities to practice speaking Tagalog. Some of the adults tended to want to use English. However, the maids and the five children, including those of Tess' brother and his wife (who also lived on the same compound), were happy to talk to Debbie in Tagalog. In the beginning, even though the children were quite young, their fluency level well surpassed hers.

While Debbie studied, I became involved in a number of things. Some invitations for outreaches came in, so I contacted Alan. I had him come to Manila when I needed him to accompany me on those outreaches. Most of these were in Bulacan, the province just north of Metro Manila, so we were home most nights, although occasionally we took longer trips.

I also took some time at the language school to do a refresher course in Tagalog which they had designed just for me. I also started my long-awaited doctoral program during this time. After much prayer and looking around, I settled on doing a doctorate in missiology at the Asia Graduate School of Theology—Philippines. This school, operated under the auspices of the Asia Theological Association, was Asia-wide with schools operating in various countries. The school was unique in that it had no resident campus, at least in the Philippines. It was actually made up of a consortium of evangelical seminaries, including APTS, with various schools hosting different programs. My program was based at the Asian Theological Seminary in Quezon City, less than three miles from where we lived.

Besides knowing that it was the leading of the Lord, and that I love to study, my only motive was to improve my missionary skills. Debbie later claimed that my missionary skills improved by simply taking the entrance exam, which I had done while we were on itineration. I did not need a doctorate for the work I was doing. Only God knew how much I would need the degree in the future.

My program followed the British educational method. There were no classes to attend, except for orientation week and one week of meetings a year or two later. The program focused on doing four tutorials, each comprising a sixty-page paper written at the doctoral level. In most cases, the subject was related to one's dissertation. A mentor is assigned to the student for each paper. Normally, the student can pick their mentor, preferably one who is an expert in the subject under study, provided that the mentor has the necessary qualifications. Once the tutorials were completed, the student would go on to the dissertation. If the student used any of the tutorials in the dissertation, the time needed to complete the dissertation could be decreased. This style of study would prove to be of great benefit to me, and I was able to use all of my tutorials in the actual dissertation. My mentor, Julie Ma, a Korean missiologist who was teaching at APTS, was an outstanding teacher who pushed me to do my best. She was willing to do anything to help me but did not tolerate sloppy work. She was the best mentor anybody could have wanted. Along the way, she and her husband, Wonsuk, became dear friends and we remain in contact with to this day.

There were many advantages to this approach to education. Since Debbie and I knew that we would not be staying in Manila once she finished language study, not having classes would save the time and expense of going back and forth to Manila. Working independently with a mentor would allow me to set my own schedule and work around ministry responsibilities. The disadvantage of this, however, is that there were fewer deadlines and no class structure that would provide greater accountability. Self-discipline was needed to ensure I took sufficient study time, and it would mean the difference between success or failure.

One other major project got underway during this time. During the late 1980s and early 1990s, an AG missionary in Brazil named Donald Stamps wrote the notes and commentary of what came to be known as the *Full Life Study Bible (FLSB)*, now known in many places as the *Fire Bible*. Stamps saw that most pastors in Brazil lacked the financial resources to build their own libraries that would support their preaching ministry for a lifetime. He realized that it would be a great help to the pastors if a one-volume commentary covering the major doctrines of Scripture could be prepared for them, so he set out to accomplish that task.

The *FLSB* was originally written in English, and initially translated into Portuguese and Spanish. By 1998, the AGWM was seeking to see this fine pastors' tool translated into languages all over the world. Every year, the missionaries that are home for itineration gather in Springfield, Missouri, for a time of refreshing, vision casting and other things, called School of Missions, which was later changed to Missionary Renewal.

While we were attending in 1998 our new area director, Bill Snider, asked me if I would be interested in overseeing the translation of the *FLSB* into Tagalog. Unbeknownst to him, I had written his predecessor, Russ Turney, several months before and expressed an interest in doing so. Russ thought it was a good idea, but he was in transition from being our area director to the regional director for the entire Asia Pacific region. The timing was not right to pursue the matter and I let it drop, especially as we were about to return to the States for itineration at that time.

Now, however, the situation was different. Life Publishers, the arm of AGWM tasked with translating, publishing and marketing the FLSB globally, wanted to do more translations into Asian languages, and was raising the funds to do so. After praying about it, Debbie and I felt led by the Lord to accept the assignment. About six months later, while we were still itinerating, I flew to St. Louis to meet the leader of Life Publishers, Gene Schachterle and his wife, Karen, for training in how to manage the project. I went into the meeting thinking that this was really a great idea. Four hours later, after grasping what would need to be done, I walked out of the meeting asking, "Lord, what am I getting myself into?" The reality is that the project would be much, much bigger than I ever dreamed.

Once we returned to Manila, I set about getting the Full Life Study Bible-Tagalog Translation Project (FLSB-TTP) underway. The first order of business was to recruit translators and editors. I used every venue possible to get the word out: minister's meetings, personal contacts and references, and even a bulletin announcement in a large church. In the end, we had about a dozen translators and another dozen served as editors. At one meeting with the leadership of the Philippines General Council of the Assemblies of God (PGCAG), I had a strong sense that I should invite Carmelita Gallardo, then serving as the General Treasurer of the PGCAG, to be the translation coordinator. Inviting Ate[1]

---

[1]Ate is an informal Tagalog term of respect that means "elder sister."

Car, as we all fondly called her, would turn out to be the best decision I made in the whole project.

We were able to find office space on the campus of Bethel Bible College in Valenzuela City, which is one of the many cities that make up the Metro Manila area. The PGCAG headquarters was also on that campus, which would make it convenient for Ate Car to work between the two offices. The office was in the building that originally housed APTS (then known as the Far East Advanced School of Theology), which started there in 1964 and moved to Baguio in 1986. I also needed to find a project secretary and soon hired Met-Met Ramos, a local girl. In time, we hired Sheryl Villagas (who we called "Ninia"), as the project grew and we realized we needed more help.

Another decision that would have huge implications was our decision to use the Tagalog Bible translation. The Philippine Bible Society (PBS) had already produced a couple of good translations, so I asked the PGCAG leadership which translation we should use. Since they were among the older generation, they decided that we should try to get approval from PBS to use the *Ang Biblia*, which was translated in the early twentieth century. When word began to spread, younger leaders became concerned about the choice made. Further research revealed that the younger generation preferred the *Mabuting Balita Biblia* (Good News Bible), which was completed in 1980 and was the most up-to-date version at that time.[2] Both translations were done from the original biblical languages. I asked Roli de la Cruz, a young Filipino scholar who was teaching at APTS, and highly respected by the PGCAG leadership, to write a letter to them and ask if they would reconsider their decision. He wrote one of the kindest, most respectful letters I have ever read, and it was well received by the leaders. Based on Roli's letter, along with hearing the voices of some of the other younger leaders, the PGCAG gladly changed their decision and opted for the modern version instead.

---

[2]This is not to be confused with the Good News Bible that was popular in the States in the 1970s.

But making good decisions can take time and that was the case here. By the time I had the project set up and ready to start, Debbie was wrapping up language studies, and we were prepared to move out of Manila.

While all of this was going on, tragedy struck my family. My mom's health had been slowly declining for a couple of years. In December 1999, she was scheduled to return to the Mayo Clinic in Minnesota for a routine checkup. The doctor felt that it would be okay for them to drive rather than fly, so that they would have transportation while they were there. They decided to take a small detour along the way and spend the night with my younger brother, Tom, who, by this time had retired from the Navy and had gone through an unfortunate divorce. He then remarried and, with his new wife and family, now lived in Clinton, Iowa. Shortly after getting up the next morning to continue their journey, mom suffered a stroke and went into a coma. She was rushed to the nearest hospital, where as it happened, Tom's wife was employed as a psychiatric nurse. By the time Dad was able to call me several hours later, about 3 a.m. in Manila, on the morning of December 5, there was no longer any hope of Mom recovering. Dad asked me to stay near the phone and wait for further developments.

Needless to say, we did not sleep much the rest of the night. We found comfort in one another and God. We also found refuge in singing the great hymns of the church, which my mother had taught since I was a child. Since December 5 was a Sunday, I stayed home from church in case Dad called. Debbie offered to stay home, but I sent her to church with one of the maids whom Debbie had just led to the Lord, in order to get her connected with the church. This left me home alone when Dad called about noon to say that Mom had just passed away. I promised we would get home as soon as we could, and he promised to wait with the funeral until we could get there.

Getting out of the Philippines, like many other countries, requires securing an exit/reentry permit, which takes a day or two to get from the Bureau of Immigration. Debbie also got sick, and we had to wait an extra day for her to be well enough to travel. Steve, Terrie and the kids had joined Dad, Tom and Lori in Clinton. They all needed time to get home, as well as make arrangements for Mom's body to be transported back to Grand Rapids for burial.

Mom knew that I loved her and I knew that she loved me, so it did not bother me that we could not get home before she died. We had had a close relationship and there were no issues that needed to be resolved. The same was true with my brothers. We all had sorrow, but not regret. She was only 67, so she died a bit young, but she went to be with the Lord, whom she had loved all of her life, so we had no complaints!

We arrived on Wednesday. True to his word, Dad scheduled one night of viewing (or wake) for Thursday night, with the funeral on Friday. Lots of family and friends turned out to comfort us. Dad later estimated that ninety percent of the members of their church came to the viewing, funeral, or both. We were really touched and comforted by their words and presence. Since the holidays were so close, we decided to stay with Dad through the holidays before returning to the Philippines.

The holidays without Mom were really hard and I broke down and cried during Christmas dinner. Nevertheless, we found comfort in God and each other. However, by this time Tom and Lori had returned to Iowa, but they stayed in touch by phone. Dad was glad that he had us staying with him during the holidays which eased his sorrow just a bit. Before we left, I told Dad that if he ever wished to remarry, that was okay with me; my brothers all said the same thing. The timing to even think about such a thing was terrible, but I felt that this was better said face-to-face than over the phone. Dad received it well. I certainly did not want any woman to replace my mother, but I also did not want Dad to be lonely. He did not seem to be the type to do well growing old alone. It was either on New Year's Day, or just after, that Debbie and I flew to Seattle to spend a couple of days with her family. They also comforted us in our sorrow. Then, we headed back across the Pacific to return to the land of our calling.

Before we left for itineration in 1998, we decided that after we returned, and Debbie completed language school, we would move to the island of Palawan, where I had done a couple of ministry tours during our first term. We would do evangelism, teach in a local Bible school and engage in some ministry to Muslims. Debbie was willing to go but never really had peace about it. While we were home itinerating, Bill Snider wrote and asked if we would consider going to the Bicol region, which comprises the southern third of the island of Luzon. I had been to the region a number of times and had a good friendship with Jesse Tan, the district superintendent. I had done one or more ministry tours with him during my first term. He was asking for missionary assistance in teaching at their small Bible school while also doing evangelism, which was exactly the type of situation for which we were looking. We delayed making a final decision until we had returned to the field. Then, I had the opportunity to take Debbie there for a weekend to get a feel of what ministry there might be like. We went for a weekend shortly after Debbie had enrolled in language school. The weekend went well except for the fact that she was robbed while riding on a jeepney when she was doing some last-minute shopping with a new friend. Despite this unfortunate experience, and after much prayer, we felt the Lord directing us to go there instead of Palawan. We made the commitment to go after Debbie completed language study, and in time for the new school year to begin in June 2000.

In May 2000, Debbie completed her language studies and it was time to pack and move to Daraga, where the Bible school was located. It was a suburb of Legaspi City, the capitol of the Bicol region, and was about twelve hours by car from Manila. In March we had made a quick trip there to attend the annual minister's convention to get acquainted with the pastors and find a place to live. At that time, Jesse told us he would not be continuing as the district superintendent. He went one step further by also leaving the Assemblies of God. While this caused us some temporary anxiety, the new superintendent, Salvador Belen, made it clear that he wanted us to come as well. We made the move about two months later.

The Bicol region comprises the southern third of the island of Luzon. The islands of Catanduanes to the east and Masbate to the west, as well as numerous smaller islands up and down both coasts were also part of the Bicol region. On Luzon, it is comprised of the provinces of Camarines Norte, Camarines Sur, Albay and Sorsogon, going from north to south. The area was quite large. Driving from the northern border to the southern tip, nearly 200 miles, took about nine hours by private vehicle. It took even more time by public transportation, which is what most pastors used, because the highway was only two lanes. Going from east to west, the distance took about three to four hours to traverse at the widest point, but it took only thirty minutes to one hour in the Legaspi area, where the land area was quite narrow going from east to west.

The local people are called Bicolanos. They have their own language, Bicol, which unfortunately, is fragmented into twenty-six dialects. Conversing sometimes required the use of Tagalog as a bridge language because some of the dialects of Bicol varied so much that people from different parts of the region could not understand one another's dialect. Additionally, the island of Masbate had their own language, Masbateño, as did the central part of Camarines Sur, where Iriganeo is spoken. The Bible is available in the Bicol language, but the translation is old and out of date. Almost all Bicolanos speak Tagalog quite well because many Filipinos from other parts of the Philippines have migrated to the Bicol region. Most of the people read the Bible in Tagalog or English. Most church services are conducted in Tagalog, which was also the language of instruction at the Bible school where we would teach. These were the main reasons we chose to not to learn Bicol. Instead, we focused instead on improving our ability in Tagalog. I must confess that I also was not really keen on trying to learn a third language.

We found a house in a nice subdivision about a ten-minute drive from the airport going one direction and ten minutes in the opposite direction to the Bible school. It also had easy access to the Pan Philippine National Highway that ran north to south through the entire region. The house had three bedrooms and a large office space in the front of the house, as well as two full, and one-half bathrooms. The house also came with two kitchens, one for cooking and the other for washing dishes, etc., which was a common feature of Filipino homes. One of the bathrooms must have been added as an afterthought. It was sandwiched in between the cooking kitchen and a small atrium in the middle of the house. It was so narrow that large people who needed to use the stool would have to sit sideways—meaning that only Filipinos could use it. Fortunately for us, the other bathrooms were larger. All in all, we liked the house and the rent fit our budget, so we signed the contract, ensuring that the house would be reserved for us when we moved.

We made the move in May, 2000, right before classes started at the Bible school. We had two summer interns from the States, Mark Carter and Matt Shultz, who made the trip with us. They helped with the move and stayed with us. Like me back in 1983, they were exploring what missionary life was all about and they spent eight weeks with us. Also, with this move, Alan Esplana came back on board as a full-time member of the team. Pedio Belaro, who had worked with me when I made past tours through Bicol and went to the same church as Alan, also joined the team. He stayed with us about seven years, some of them full-time, depending on our needs and financial resources.

Debbie said that I would get much more work out of her if I provided her with air-conditioning. The house did not have central air and was not sufficiently insulated to allow for it. I went out and purchased four new and one used wall mounted, single room air-conditioners, which cost a total about $2,000. With the landlord's permission, we hired someone to cut holes in the walls of the bedrooms and office space where the air conditioners would be placed. We also had to install support brackets and steel bars on the outside of the air-conditioners to prevent thieves from pushing in the air conditioners and getting inside the house.

Along with every other house in the subdivision, the property was enclosed with a perimeter wall that had glass shards embedded in the top, along with concertina wire strung along the top to reduce the possibility of break-ins. Taking basic security precautions is simply a way of life of any missionary living in the non-western world. Most other homes in the subdivision also had guard dogs, but we decided not to get one due to the lack of space outdoors. Since I was asthmatic at the time, having an animal living inside was not a healthy option for me.

We had no sooner gotten settled than it was time to start classes at the Bible school. From its inception in 1914, the leadership of the Assemblies of God saw that it was important to train leaders to conserve the fruits of revival. The AG missionaries carried this philosophy to the Philippines when they came. The school in Daraga, called Evangel Bible College, began in the 1960s. It was moved to Daraga, a suburb of Legaspi, in the early 1990s, when a missionary named Wes Weekley raised the needed funds. An old broom factory was purchased and converted into a Bible school. Despite its auspicious name, it was only a three-year institute with an enrollment of about twenty-five to thirty students per semester in the years we were there. The main building was a two-story structure that featured several rooms which were converted into classrooms and dormitories. It had a chapel on the main floor and a larger room used for district-wide meetings on the second floor, with the school's library directly below it. One room was used for the Bible school office, and another room served as the headquarters for the Bicol Region District Council of the Assemblies of God (BRDCAG). Men's and women's bathrooms were on the main floor, which was a good idea since the city's water pressure was often too low to get water to the second floor. There was a rooftop apartment above the second floor that had a bathroom, and on good days, enough running water to take a bath with a bucket and scoop. The kitchen and dining hall were in a separate building across the way. We also found badly needed space on campus to store the sound equipment and literature used by our evangelistic team.

By the time we arrived, the flooring in the large meeting room on the second floor needed replacing. When I asked for an estimate on what it would cost to do it, two of our pastor-instructors made up a list of costs. Their calculations were so far off I determined that I would no longer ask preachers to estimate construction costs! Fortunately, God had blessed us with extra funds, so the cost was not a problem. When we tore up the old wooden floor, we discovered that termites had done a thorough job on it. We concluded that the only reason the floor was still in place was because angels and the remaining termites were holding hands!

Since all faculty members were part-time and pastored local churches, each class convened only once a week for three hours at a time. Most of our students were single and quite young. At the time, most Filipinos were graduating from high school at age 16. Naturally, many of them were quite immature and lacked the discipline that serious study at a Bible school required. That meant teachers had to be patient. Also, the school had to enforce a fairly strict daily regimen to help ensure that the students got the most from their studies and were also involved in ministry on the weekends.

Due to a chronic lack of funds, few library books were available. Over the years, the school had been able to pull together a library of about 1,000 volumes, mainly from donations. Instructors learned to make do with what was available. The language barrier was a major problem. Nearly all of the books were in English, which most of the students did not read well. We donated a couple of English/Tagalog dictionaries shortly after we arrived so that the students could look up English words that they did not know. The dictionaries became some of the most used books in the library! We also donated books from our personal library, and as resources allowed, bought books for the school to help as best we could. We included the *Full Life Study Bible*, when it became available in

Tagalog. However, the lack of theological literature in the Tagalog language remains a great challenge to this day.

The backbone and key to success of any school is always the faculty. Most of the faculty were graduates of EBC. The academic dean, Nelson Verona, was the exception. He was a Bicolano who had moved to Manila many years before. He pastored there and travelled about twelve hours one way by bus to handle his responsibilities at the school. The president, Danny Romero, actually pastored a church about forty-three miles north of Manila. He had an even longer trek to Daraga, which meant he did not come often.

Classes began in June with the onset of the rainy season, and concluded in March, at the start of the hottest season of the year. Teaching assignments were not made until the teachers' meeting at the beginning of the year, giving us only a short time to prepare. I was asked to teach a course in Romans and Galatians for one semester, and hermeneutics (how to interpret the Bible) in the second. Debbie was asked to teach Pentecostal Foundations and English. At one point, she volunteered to teach Church History since no one else was available, even though she has no academic background that area. She also taught other courses as the years passed. I taught for only one year, and concluded that continuing to teach was not God's will for me. Debbie, whose teaching gifts were readily apparent to all who know her well, taught at least one or two courses every semester for a total of nine years. She also succeeded Romero as president in 2003 and served until 2009. That story, along with the continued development of our evangelistic ministry and many other things, is told in the next few chapters.

CHAPTER 11

The Early Years in Bicol
(2000-2004)

The move to Bicol represented a tremendous change in the geography of our evangelistic ministry. We felt led by the Lord to limit the geographical focus of our ministry to the Bicol region rather than continuing to travel to other parts of the nation. This would allow us to serve one region well, and gave us the opportunity to serve the various pastors on multiple occasions. This also gave us the chance to develop good relationships with many of them. Conversely, it also meant that others would be needed to serve other parts of the nation. For that, I teamed up with another missionary couple, Gerald and Donna Johnson (no relation), who founded the Evangelist's Training Center in Davao City, on the island of Mindanao. For several years, I spent a week there, sometimes with Debbie sometimes alone, helping them train Filipino evangelists from all over the islands.

Focusing on one region also provided the opportunity for us to really think through our ministry philosophy and what partnership with the PGCAG area leadership would look like. Early on, I found myself asking, "What do we want to leave behind when we leave?" No missionary is ever permanent anywhere, and we had no idea how long the Lord would have us there. Since we realized that maintaining an evangelistic ministry was quite expensive, and likely beyond the reach of the churches, we determined to focus our efforts on leading people to Christ and seeing them channeled into new or existing churches. In that sense, the evangelistic ministry was like the scaffolding on a construction site. Once the project was complete, the scaffolding could be removed. This decision would prove to be among the most important and long lasting that we would make while we were there.

By the time we moved to Bicol, I had been doing evangelism in the Philippines for several years, and had pretty well settled into a routine of how we conducted our evangelistic outreaches. Innovation has never been my greatest gift and Filipinos are quite comfortable with doing the same thing the same way over and over again. They easily understood why we did things the way we did. So, we did not see the need to greatly change our style over the years, although we continually finetuned our approach as needed, revising our manual as we gained more experience or for other reasons. We also gave local pastors the opportunity to have input as we went along. We revised the manual every year or so to reflect ministry realities that called for minor changes.

One area that required constant attention was finances. Coming from a country with a much higher standard of living than the Filipinos created the impression, real or imagined, that we had plenty of money. My missiological training at AGTS had helped me form a philosophy of investing finances in our missions' activities in a way designed to help the PGCAG churches, but not to the point of doing things for them that they could do for themselves. For example, we knew that purchasing and maintaining a vehicle and sound equipment for the ministry, as well as paying the salaries and expenses of the team members, was beyond the ability of the churches to provide, at least at the time. Providing some of the food for the evangelistic team and the local church workers who served as counselors, as well as providing a place for us to stay when we were at a church, however, was another matter and we challenged the churches participating to do this. Maintaining a good balance and communicating with the pastors, however, was not always easy and required the wisdom of Solomon to accomplish! As time went on, we encouraged the churches to pick up more and more of the financial burden. This became easier as we developed closer relationships with the pastors and they got to know our hearts, but the issue never entirely went away. We wanted to serve the local churches without creating an unhealthy dependence on us.

One major change that we did make was in the timing of our follow-up on those who expressed an interest in following Jesus in our rallies. In the beginning, we let the pastor decide when follow-up would be done, and they normally opted to wait until the week after we left. In time, however, I read a study that indicated that immediate follow-up brought better long-term results. Waiting gave the Devil time to sow doubts in people's minds about their salvation. When I realized this, we began challenging the pastors to begin follow-up while we were still there. Change is always hard, and we met with some resistance in the beginning, but eventually the pastors became used to doing things differently. However, my team members were often the only ones doing the follow-up while we were there. I did not participate in the follow-up myself because I felt that the people we visited would be more likely to open up to other Filipinos than to an American. I also used the time for preparing to teach my class, writing my dissertation or handling other responsibilities. In retrospect, I do not think I set a good example by demanding of others what I did not do myself; I would not recommend that others follow my example in this regard.

The churches received us well. In the thirteen years that we served there, we conducted an average of 40-45 three-night evangelistic rallies per year. We were on the road nearly every weekend except for holidays, or about 120-150 nights a year. Through trial and error, we came to the decision that three members of our team, besides Debbie and me, was optimal to do the work that needed to be done. Over the years, local Filipinos named Pedio Belaro, Edwin Perillo, Randy Bromahon, Zaqueo (Bong) Florendo, Joash Coronel and Ronald Buenconsejo served with Alan, Debbie and I, either on a part-time or full-time basis. However, only Alan, who married and had five children over the years we were there, remained with us the entire time. We loved them all and they became like younger brothers, or even sons to us. Randy and Ronald came to know the Lord through our ministry and were invited to join the team after they got saved. We made every effort to mentor them in the faith and the ministry.

Debbie's schedule at the Bible school, especially after she became president in 2003, often precluded her from going to the rallies with us. This afforded me a lot of informal times with the team. We traveled thousands of miles together, slept on the same church floors, ate the same food at the same dinner tables, played a lot of basketball, and when the situation demanded, we took our baths in the same river. On at least one occasion the guys had to pull my flipflops out of the mud for me. I also sent several of them through driver's education and they practiced using our STL vehicle. I have never been a father, but I do understand the nervousness parents experience when turning over the keys to a new, inexperienced driver. I eventually had Alan take them out for practice sessions and we never had any problem.

Living among the people in a provincial area gave us an unparalleled opportunity to develop close relationships with PGCAG leaders. The PGCAG was divided into twenty geographical districts that consisted of a district superintendent, assistant superintendent, secretary and treasurer. Each district was further divided into sections that were overseen by a presbyter and assistant presbyter, etc. Each district also had a number of department heads for youth ministries, Christian education and so on. The district presbytery, then, was made up of the district leaders, department heads and presbyters.

The entire Bicol region was made up of one district.[1] There were six sections, which were later divided into ten, and about 130 churches. Given the wide geography of the district, and that over 100 pastors served these churches, we quickly realized that we could not possibly form close relationships with everyone. Still, we did try to at least know them all.

---

[1] In 2018, the PGCAG divided the region into two districts to better oversee the growth and development of the churches.

Since the district office was at the Bible school, we saw the district and sectional leaders quite often, and we forged close relationships with many of them. We became their friends, confidants, and in some cases, their mentors, since many of them were younger than we were. As we settled in to work among them, I recognized that we would not only hear about the good things that the Lord was doing among them, but we would also hear of their struggles, trials and challenges in interpersonal relationships. I determined to keep my ears open, my heart soft and my mouth closed. By and large, I think I succeeded, although certainly not perfectly. Filipinos, as a whole, are shy about sharing their innermost problems and struggles with cultural outsiders. But with time and lots of love, they eventually looked past our white skin and strange ways and adopted us as their own. While many of them spoke English quite well, most of them preferred to speak to us in Tagalog most of the time, especially when talking about heart issues. It reinforced to us the reality that while Filipinos do like English, they love their own languages. Since ministry flows from relationships, we came to understand that knowing the language, culture and people well was critical to our success as missionaries.

Not only were relationships with Filipinos critical, so were relationships with other missionaries, both within our own mission as well as missionaries with other groups. Except for the years 2002-2005 when we had another AG missionary couple working with us, we were the only AG missionaries in the entire region. Not more than a few months after we arrived there, God began to speak to me about the unity of the body of Christ. We did not know any pastors outside of the PGCAG, and therefore, had no influence over them. We did know a couple of missionaries, Bob and Koleen French and their daughters, who lived in Naga City, about two hours drive north of Legaspi. We also knew Bruce and Eileen Gladigau, who lived in Legaspi. The Frenches were Americans serving with an interdenominational mission called World

Team. The Gladigaus were independent missionaries from Australia, but had an AG background.

When we shared my burden for unity in the body with the Frenches, they were in immediate agreement that we needed to do something. They knew other missionaries in the region, and we knew the Gladigaus, so we contacted everybody, and about three weeks later, we held an organizational meeting at a hotel restaurant in Legaspi. Together we formed the Bicol Expats Evangelical Fellowship (BEEF). We decided to meet on a monthly basis in one of our homes, rotating every month, usually between Naga and Legaspi. In order to focus on our unity in Christ, we agreed that any doctrinal issue that would cause division in the group would be outlawed for discussion during our group meeting times. At no point did we ever ask anyone to change doctrinal positions, nor did anyone ever expect it of us.

We initially discussed doing ministry projects together, such as church planting. Then we were faced with the issue as to what group such a church would belong. We quickly realized that this was not a particularly good idea. What did happen was that individual group members banded together to do ministry projects on occasion. Two couples, who had six children between them, formed a boys' and girls' club for their children. On one occasion, we loaned our sound equipment to some Baptists friends for an outreach they were doing. We ended up doing significant ministry with the Frenches for several years. That story will be told in the next chapter.

Instead of working on projects we focused on fellowship, food, and prayer. Most of the couples had children who were home schooled, so they were included too. Debbie and I became aunt and uncle to other peoples' children. Koleen French was the original coordinator, with several of us eventually taking turns at organizing the group over the years. We met monthly for nine years, until 2009. Our meetings were more sporadic after that, as many moved on to other places, and the number of missionaries in the region decreased.

Not all of the missionaries in the region chose to participate, but most did as their schedules allowed. We came from a variety of national backgrounds with Americans, Australians, British, Canadian, Austrian and Romanians all participating at one time or another. Denominationally, we had Baptists of various sorts, Pentecostals, Lutherans, Brethren and independents all praying together. Since the Frenches were from an interdenominational mission, years passed before Debbie and I ever figured out that their church background was rather eclectic. Since they loved Jesus, it did not matter! The differences did not make a difference to us!

The results were stupendous. Because we focused on what united us rather than what divided us, we created a safe atmosphere where group members were able to forge close friendships. As our trust in one another grew, we were able to open up and share our hurts and our pains as well as our joys and victories. Many years have now passed, and most of us have moved on to other ministries and other locations, but the warm memories are still there, and in some cases, we are still in contact with one another. Back in 2010, while Debbie and I were home on furlough, two couples and their children came to visit us overnight at the same time! We had ten people in a house with only one bathroom!

There were two occasions when we needed to be involved in disaster relief. A couple of months before we moved, and the year after we arrived, Mt. Mayon, the most active volcano in the Philippines, and located less than ten miles from our house, erupted. It spewed volcanic ash all over our province. Tens of thousands of people were temporarily displaced and were housed in school buildings that served as relocation centers—even while classes were in session. Because the area is largely agrarian, mainly rice, and because rice grows above the ground, millions of dollars of rice crops were destroyed by the volcanic ash. Fortunately, there was little property damage, and almost no loss of life. However, the toxic air from the falling ash caused lots of respiratory problems.

With lots of help from AGWM and our supporters in the States, we were able to help provide food and other items needed by those in the relocation centers. We also did evangelistic outreaches in these centers, and people came to know the Lord. In the end, two churches were planted as a result of these efforts. We rejoiced that we could be there when people needed us. While we could not meet every need, we were able to help. That help was deeply appreciated by those affected.

As we were getting settled in Bicol, the *Full Life Study Bible* Tagalog Translation Project (*FLSB*-TTP) was getting underway in Manila. About the same time, Carmelita Gallardo, left her position as the General Treasurer of the PGCAG. She devoted herself full-time to running the project's office on the Bethel Bible College campus. On a normal day, she and the two secretaries were the only ones there and I communicated with them by email and phone as necessary. The translators and editors normally worked out of their own homes or churches, since many of them were pastors, and I did the same in Daraga.

Since LIFE Publishers had only completed a few translations at that time, they did not have a well-developed system to handle the project. They gave me a lot of leeway on how to handle the task as I saw fit. Since I had never done this before, we had a few months of trial and error before we settled into an organizational pattern that worked for us.

When I interviewed prospective translators, I tested their abilities by asking them to translate one of the articles in the *FLSB* on the Baptism in the Holy Spirit, which was only one of seventy-seven articles in that study Bible. I also asked them to time how long it took them to do it. This allowed me to give them translation assignments that corresponded to the amount of time they could dedicate to the project every week. Ate Car had done a lot of translating by working for the International Correspondence Institute (ICI). Now known as Global University in America, ICI was a worldwide AGWM literature and distance education ministry. Ate Car worked for ICI for over thirty years, so she evaluated the quality of the translators' work.

Once we had the translators and editors chosen, we were set to begin. It became my job to make out the assignments, determining how much a translator should be expected to accomplish in a two-week period. Once I had done this, Ate Car would then make the assignments to the various translators. Once the translators turned in their assignments, two editors, plus Ate Car, were then assigned to each piece of work to be sure it was done well. Since some of the translators and editors did not have computers, we added steps where the project secretaries encoded the translators' and editors' work into the computer before going on to the next step. Ate Car was an excellent administrator and a master of the details. In the end, she developed a nine-step process that each assignment went through in order to ensure that we produced the best work that we could possibly do. She became the heart and soul of the project and no one, including me, invested more time and effort in the work than she did, often taking work home with her at night.

Since the translators' and editors' assignments were due every two weeks, we decided to call a team meeting at the Manila office every other Tuesday to review assignments, give out new ones, and solve problems as they occurred. This also provided a sense that we were all part of one team, which was important because Filipino culture is group oriented. The editors met during the day. Since the editors worked in teams of two, they would often come to the office to work together on their assignments. The translators came in the evening, which meant that those of us who had to attend both meetings had quite a long day.

To facilitate a great atmosphere at these meetings, we provided lunch for the editors and supper for the translators. There was a local hamburger chain and a local pizza joint that provided delivery service. We became regular customers of both, eating hamburgers and spaghetti for lunch and pizza at night, which added to my already well-padded waist line.

For me, however, attending these meetings came at some personal cost, but we all felt that I really needed to be there as much as possible. I had to fly to Manila on Mondays, be in meetings all day on Tuesday, and fly home on Wednesday. While the project budget covered my travel, Monday was normally our day off, and I had to give up at least part of it to travel. This is a violation of the biblical concept of the Sabbath and I do not recommend following my example here. It also meant time away from Debbie, but we had counted the cost in this regard before we agreed to take on the project. Still, we missed each other since she rarely came with me. However, the fact that these meetings accomplished a lot, and we had such a great time being together, mitigated some of the cost.

We learned to deal with problems as they arose. One problem that arose early in the project is the dialectical differences in the Tagalog that is spoken in various parts of the country. Compounded with this is the 187 languages and dialects which are spoken in the Philippines. For many, including the Bicolanos, Tagalog was their second language, meaning that they normally did not speak it as well as a native Tagalog speaker. As with many languages, Tagalog also has two levels, the Tagalog of the common people and the more formal (or deep) Tagalog used in speeches, poetry, sermons and formal writing. Since the *FLSB* was considered formal writing, proper etiquette would call for using the deeper Tagalog. But those who spoke Tagalog as a second, or even third, language often did not know the deep Tagalog words. Further, since the deeper Tagalog was not preferred by the younger generation of native speakers, we could not follow the normal etiquette. All of the translators, except one or two, were native Tagalog speakers. They tended to want to use the deeper Tagalog, especially since Tagalog is such a beautiful, poetic language. But they also agreed that if we wanted to appeal to the broadest range of Filipinos as possible, we had to use words that most Filipinos could understand.

We took three steps to ensure that this happened. First, the *Mabuting Balita Biblia*, the Tagalog version of the Bible that we used, was geared toward the same broader reader audience we were targeting, and did not use as much deep Tagalog as the older version we had considered using. We asked the translators to try to use the same vocabulary as the biblical text in translating the commentary, notes and articles of the *FLSB*.

Since this did not quite solve the entire problem, the second step was to have me review every assignment and circle words that I did not know. By the time we started the project I had been speaking Tagalog for six years. While I was doing well in the language, I still lacked a lot of the vocabulary that a native speaker would know. In other words, I was like those Filipinos who also spoke Tagalog as a second or third language. Once I reviewed an assignment, it went back to the editors to see if words needed to be changed. Doing this had the additional advantage of helping me keep tabs on the project while improving my Tagalog! Third, we hired Filipino BBC students to read the assignments to help ensure the readability of the text. Once it was published, the *FLSB* Tagalog became quite popular nationwide, suggesting that we had largely achieved our goal.

As the project grew, we had to grow and change procedures along with it, adding personnel to meet the needs. In addition to adding a second secretary, we also hired a young BBC graduate named Leophe Orosco to handle some special aspects of the project. Her main contribution was reviewing the *FLSB*'s center referencing system, which is a standard part of most study Bibles. The center referencing system noted in the center column between the biblical texts Bible verses that had similar words related to other verses elsewhere in Scripture (i.e. the Old Testament citations in the New Testament). The problem is, these references were keyed to specific words, and these words are different when translated into other languages. This required Leophe to look up thousands of biblical references and compare them to the Tagalog Bible, adding, deleting or changing the references as necessary. This became a long, tedious process, but Leophe later testified that she knew the Bible much better than before she came to work for us!

The *FLSB* also includes a concordance of several hundred pages. Due to the immense workload that maxed our people and computer availability, I decided to do the concordance last—and lived to regret it. This part of the project proved to be a colossal challenge, one that Leophe undertook once she finished the center referencing system. Again, translating from one language to another can be a real headache. First, the ranges of word meanings can be different. For example, the English word "later" could mean later today, tomorrow, next week, or next year. The closest Tagalog equivalent, *mamaya*, can only mean "later today." Other words are needed to express the concept of later periods of time.

A more serious problem is English may have one word to express a concept, but Tagalog may have two or more words that mean the same thing, or vice versa. For example, the English word "love" has two equivalents in Tagalog "*mahal*" and "*pag-ibig.*" This meant that Leophe had to look up every single Scripture reference to love in the Tagalog Bible and separate them into two headings, instead of one, for the Tagalog concordance. This was extremely tedious and time-consuming. Debbie, who valiantly served as the project's technical editor as well as helping Ate Car with the financial records, encountered major challenges in getting all of Leophe's work into a format that Life Publishers could use for layout. Thankfully, they persevered and did it well.

The deadline for finishing our part of the project was June 30, 2002. We realized that if we had any hope of making the deadline, we had to do something drastic. We pushed all of our other work aside, and temporarily relocated to Metro Manila, to devote full time to the project. Fortunately, we found housing on the BBC campus right next door to the office. All of the office staff, including us, averaged twelve- to fourteen-hour workdays, except Sundays, for six weeks, but we still missed the deadline by twenty-three days. When Life Publishers heard about what we were doing, they graciously extended the deadline.

Finally, our part was done. We celebrated with a big party in a nice restaurant for all of the forty-three people who served in the project one way or another. We also treated the office staff to a weekend retreat at a nice resort just outside of Manila. We were all exhausted but happy.

After we were finished, Life took the files we sent and the copy of the *Mabuting Balita Biblia* provided by the Philippine Bible Society (PBS) and did the layout in their Springfield, MO, office. The layout files were then emailed back to us for a final proofread, since nobody in Springfield could read Tagalog. When the layout was finished, they had 10,000 copies printed by a company in Japan. They had the bookbinding done in Indonesia before shipping them on to us. All this was because it was the cheapest way to do it, but the entire project still cost Life Publishers about $162,000 to produce. Also, while all this was going on, we responded to a request from Life to give a detailed explanation of the project so that they could improve and help other projects to improve. We produced a small booklet entitled, *Pursuing the Dream: How We Translated the Full Life Study Bible into Tagalog*, which Life used for years. In that way, the fruit of our labor was multiplied.

Finally, in January 2004, representatives from Life Publishers and PBS, joined with as many of the *FLSB*-TTP team that were available, and launched the Tagalog *Full Life Study Bible* at a special celebration in Manila. We were joined by the ICI team, who would handle the marketing. About ten years later, a second printing of over 6,000 copies was done due to popular demand. As of 2018, over 12,000 copies have been sold all over the nation and sales remain strong. Only God knows how many people have come to Christ and been discipled by pastors using this wonderful tool. This was my first venture into publishing. Little did I know that it would not be my last, nor would it be the end of my work with Life Publishers and the *Full Life Study Bible*.

CHAPTER 12

Early Years in Bicol
2000-2004 (Continued)

While all of these ministries were going on, I continued to work on my doctoral dissertation, which in itself, was a major undertaking. Since my master's thesis (see chapter 9) was a study on the witchcraft, divination and other animistic practices of the Waray people of Leyte-Samar, I decided to build on that work. There was not enough space in the thesis to provide a biblical response to these practices, so I decided that this would be the focus of my dissertation.

The doctoral program that I was in was based in Manila (see chapter 10). With no classes in this kind of program, which reflected the British style of education, the focus of the program was based on writing four sixty-page papers, called tutorials, and a dissertation. Since all tutorials could also be include in the dissertation itself, I was able to blend these two aspects of the program into one. Before writing the first tutorial, I had to write a dissertation proposal detailing what I planned to study. This had to be approved by a committee before I continued. The first tutorial paper then dealt with a review of all relevant literature on the subject. The next tutorial was to write a history of the AG churches in the region because I needed to understand what it was about the gospel that appealed to the Waray people, even though the number of Christians was less than one percent of the total Waray population at the time.

I scoured the bookstores and seminary and university libraries in Manila and Baguio to get the materials I needed. Then I spent hundreds of hours reading and notetaking, building a research file which would be the foundation of the dissertation. To do all of this successfully along with my other work, I had to discipline my time to be sure that I had the time I needed. Being a committed life-long learner, I had established a practice of taking a box of books along whenever we traveled for our evangelistic rallies or anything else. I turned the driving over to the team members so I could study while we were on the road. When I found something I needed to note, I marked it. Alan would transcribe what I marked onto four by six-inch index cards that were filed by subject. Other team members helped as well, saving me innumerable hours of work.

Near the end of 2001, I was ready to do the required field research (the third tutorial). I studied the religious attitudes of the local Waray, and the pastors and churches of the AG. I also needed to interview the pastors about the history and work of the AG in the area. This required preparing two questionnaires, which were then translated into Waray. I hired and trained a team of researchers to interview the over 900 respondents that would be required to do accurate research. The researchers had to be reasonably proficient in English, as well as in Waray and Tagalog. An Australian AG missionary in the area helped us select the researchers, and I think we ended up with eight or ten of them. Except for one or two all were single. Some of my researchers were pastors who took a short leave from their churches to help us. The rest of the team were recent Bible school graduates or students.

We divided into two teams, one headed by Debbie and the other by me. We managed to borrow a second car from another missionary in the area because we needed to travel to various parts of the Leyte/Samar region. Splitting into two teams would allow us to do the research quicker. All of the interviewees were chosen by a random selection process that called for selecting the communities in which they lived, and then further dividing up the communities to come up with the respondents needed. A similar process was used for selecting the members of the AG churches. One of the areas where Debbie's team planned to go was controlled by communist rebels, who would not take kindly to strangers coming into their area. The team decided that the research was not worth dying for and decided not to go. I gladly sent them elsewhere.

All in the all, we were on the road for six grueling weeks. While we were doing this, we rented another vehicle for our evangelistic team in Bicol, and Alan ran the ministry while we were gone. Ate Car took care of the *FLSB* project without much help from me, while Debbie had to reschedule her classes at the Bible school. In all, it was an incredible experience that resulted in a lot of valuable data that gave me many insights on the religious values of the people. Once the data was collected, we went home and I spent the next several months sorting, analyzing and interpreting the data. I compiled it into an amazing fifty-seven tables of information in the dissertation!

When this was completed, the next phase was to intensely study the Bible on these issues and bring biblical truth to the results of the research. This also took many months of prayer, study, thinking, writing and rewriting. Once that was completed, Debbie and I spent several additional months putting all of the parts of the dissertation together into one seamless manuscript, rewriting and editing the entire manuscript several times to produce the best possible work we could. I could not have done this well without Debbie's help. Also, my mentor Julie Ma, was involved every step of the way. Finally, in February 2004, I defended my dissertation before an appointed committee—and passed! About six weeks later, the night before my 47th birthday, I walked the graduation line. It was time to celebrate!

The impact on our ministry was profound. I preached hundreds of sermons on subjects studied in the dissertation. I also taught a number of seminars on God's response to witchcraft, sorcery, divination and many other related subjects. I developed and taught a ministry model, based on the work of other scholars. It called for a power encounter that dealt with signs and wonders, a truth encounter that taught the truth about God and the demonic nature of animistic practices, and a love encounter that focused on being the Body of Christ. All of this pointed to an allegiance encounter with Jesus Christ, who alone is Savior and Lord.

In 2006, I published a cell group series on these issues for the Asia Pacific Media Ministries of the AG in Manila, and it sold at least 1,000 copies. In 2013, I published the dissertation under the title, *Theology in Context: A Case Study in the Philippines*. To date, around 2,000 copies have gone all over the Philippines and other parts of Asia. I have also published a few journal articles on the subject. Also, in 2006 I was invited to teach a course on the subject at APTS, where I had first met Debbie a decade before. Ultimately, ministry opportunities have come our way that would not have happened had I not pursued doctoral studies. But now, I am getting too far ahead of my story!

When we were in the States for itineration in 1998-1999, a friend prophesied over me that I would be in leadership. I did not think about it much at the time, but apparently the Holy Spirit did not forget. By the end of 2001, I was leading an evangelistic team and leading the *FLSB* Tagalog project. Around November of that year, while we were doing the field research, our area director called and asked me to take one of the top leadership positions in the field, that of the Country Moderator, as the missionary serving in that capacity was retiring.

Bill Snider was the AGWM area director for the Philippines, Indonesia, Malaysia, Singapore, East Timor and Borneo. While we did not have missionaries in all of these countries, part of his job was to also represent the AGWM to the AG leaders in all of these countries. Like other countries all over the world, there were enough missionaries in the Philippines to organize a field fellowship. The field fellowships in each country were under the leadership of a Country Moderator.[1]

---

[1] The title of the job was not the same in all places.

One of the issues we had to think through was how I could possibly take on another responsibility. Neither the *FLSB* Tagalog project nor my dissertation were finished yet, but Bill could not wait. Debbie and I took a week or two to pray over the matter and the Holy Spirit indicated that he would be pleased for me to take the job. I was to trust him to help me to balance or delegate my other responsibilities. With a bit of fear and trepidation, we accepted his invitation and were installed at the annual field meeting that December.

We had about fifty-five to sixty career missionaries, along with several short-termers, working all over the Philippines at that time. The position called for handling a lot of administrative responsibilities, including working with the field business manager and our office in Manila. I was also responsible for chairing the field executive committee's bi-monthly meeting. Along with Bill, I also represented the field fellowship to the leaders of the PGCAG, which meant relating to, and interacting with, the top PGCAG leaders. The position did not have much actual authority, which did not bother me at all, but it did carry a lot of influence with both the missionaries and the Filipinos.

Beyond these basic responsibilities, and within the boundaries of what authority I did have, I was free to create my own job description. In this time period, I led the effort to review our overall field strategy. I also received a number of invitations to speak at district conventions and I accepted as many as I could. I also had the opportunity to initiate and develop, along with the PGCAG leadership and fellow missionaries Michael and Sharyl Langford, a pilot project for ministering to Muslims in the southern part of the country. The Langfords had been reaching out to Muslims for years and welcomed this new opportunity. A number of Muslims came to Christ in the years that the project functioned.

The Country Moderator's job called for a lot of travel, mainly back and forth to Manila. I also traveled to all parts of the Philippines, and a few times to one of the countries under Bill's leadership. In many cases, I was able to combine this work with the bi-weekly *FLSB* Tagalog project meetings, or trips to libraries for research or travel to Baguio to consult with my mentor. These responsibilities created an opportunity, and a need, for Alan to step up and lead the evangelistic team, which he did brilliantly.

This job also gave me the opportunity to reflect on, and participate in, the ministry partnership of the AGWM and PGCAG at a national level. The goal of the partnership was to work together to accomplish the Great Commission in the Philippines. Since ministry flows from relationships, I invested a lot of time with local Filipino leaders over coffee or a meal, just sharing fellowship as well as working together. I learned to love and respect them and they reciprocated. When difficult issues came up, we had the relationships in place to deal with most of the problems successfully.

The position also called for spending a lot of time with fellow missionaries. Part of my job was to work with them in getting approval for building projects, funds from BGMC, STL or Light-for-the-Lost. We also had the opportunity for planning social events, like the annual Thanksgiving celebration, and for a time, monthly prayer meetings for those in Manila. The biggest event of the year was the annual field meeting, which I have already mentioned, which took place over the New Year's holiday until 2006, when we moved it to early June. The annual meeting involved a combination of business, retreat (including youth and children's ministries) and fellowship. It was normally held at a hotel or resort. We had special guest speakers for all of the above. Altogether, we normally had about 100 people participating, which made for a lot of work to pull it off well. The Manila office staff did most of work under the leadership of the business manager, but I had responsibilities as well, mainly in chairing the business session and overseeing the adult program. One year, we even had a baptismal service because some of our missionary kids (MKs) wanted to be baptized with the AGMF family present. Their parents did the baptizing. We had some great meetings.

Since missionaries are as human as anybody, I was occasionally called upon to work with Bill in resolving conflicts between missionaries, or between missionaries and PGCAG leaders. In most cases, we found successful solutions or were at least able to manage the tension, but these situations were never fun. One of the greatest pleasures of the job was just working with Bill and his wife, Kim. They were great leaders and served as our area directors for nineteen years. Our philosophy of missions, partnership and leadership were quite similar and we worked well together.

It may be fair to ask how I managed all of these responsibilities. The truth is that I thoroughly enjoyed having diverse responsibilities. Doing all of them required a constant juggling act, but I am reasonably good at multi-tasking and achieving the goals that I set. On the other hand, there were some negative aspects of such a hectic lifestyle that would not become apparent for a number of years. That story will be told in another chapter.

In the Moderator's role, I was greatly aided by the entire office staff in Manila, especially the office secretary, Susan Margallo, who also served as my secretary. I worked well with missionary Mike Williams, our mission's business manager, and later with his successor, Sheree Moon. They all made my job fun. Carmelita Gallardo, as mentioned earlier, was my right-hand person at the *FLSB* Tagalog project office and more than any other person, deserves credit for the project going as well as it did. As I mentioned earlier, Alan did a great job with the evangelistic team. He also made sure that our electric bill got paid, did our banking, cleaned and maintained our truck, and took care of a lot of other routine, time consuming tasks. His friendship, integrity and work ethic were invaluable to us.

However, I am happy to confess that I only succeeded because I had great support from Debbie. She participated in the evangelistic rallies when she could, edited my dissertation, did her part on the *FLSB* Tagalog project, and filled her role well as the Country Moderator's wife. She was just a great wife and partner in a multitude of ways.

While Debbie did all of the above, her main passion and focus was teaching at Evangel Bible College. After three good years on the faculty, she succeeded Danny Romero as president in 2003. At that point, she had no formal ministerial credentials, but neither did most of the other missionary wives. However, the position required her to be credentialed, so the BRDCAG gave her credentials until she could complete the requirements for the first level of credentials with the AG USA. She was eventually ordained in 2016.

Debbie is the most passionate Pentecostal I have ever known, coveting the daily presence of Jesus in her life, and she attacked her new position with great zeal. For Debbie, spiritual formation was of equal importance as academics, if not more so. Noting that some graduates had failed miserably in personal aspects of their lives not long after finishing EBC, she decided to implement a mentoring program to help students deal with personal issues, either in their background or in coping with daily life. She wrote a series of lessons to serve as a guide, and the mentoring sessions were done during chapel on Thursdays. The faculty was eager to help and each was given two or three mentees, normally divided by gender. The students responded quite well, and I think many were helped over the years that we were there. Since all Bible colleges also serve as "bridal colleges," she also developed a pre-marital counseling program that she used for those wanting help as they prepared for married life after the ceremony.

Most Filipino Pentecostals follow the Catholic tradition of having godparents when they marry or have children. I think every student that married while Debbie was president asked us to serve as godparents, as did others with whom we had close relationships. We lost track of how many godchildren we have long ago. Being a godparent is not cheap, as they are normally expected to help pay for the wedding. We determined a set amount that we gladly gave to every couple, although we occasionally padded it if the couple was especially close to us. To date, we have not heard any complaints.

Debbie loved working with the faculty members—who are the backbone of any school. These wonderful people often served without pay when there was no money. At one point, one long time faculty member and Debbie went through the entire alumni list and concluded that an amazing eighty-six percent of the graduates were actively involved in ministry. Most of them were in Bicol, but some had moved to other parts of the Philippines—and to other parts of the world. While all glory belongs to God, much credit must go to the faithful faculty who have served EBC since its founding in 1964.

In short, Debbie was a busy woman! Like me, she could not have done all that she did without help. In the Philippines, maintaining a clean and well-ordered home is much more time consuming than in the States. Since missionaries are considered to be in a high social class, they are expected to hire maids to help with the housework, or help care for children, and are usually available at a reasonable cost. While one maid caused us some problems and had to be dismissed after only a few months, all of the rest who have served in our house have been a blessing to us. Several of them were pastor's wives who had ministry responsibilities of their own, so they well understood our lives and priorities. While Debbie certainly oversaw the household and supervised the maids, their taking over many of the household chores allowed her to give most of her time to ministry.

Another factor was that God chose not to give us any biological children—we probably married too late in life for that. While this has been a painful reality to bear for both of us at times, we both recognize that having children would have taken more time away from ministry.

Help also came in the form of an AG missionary couple that served with us for three years. I first met Ray and Deborah Miller in 1985 when I preached at a church they were pastoring in Sparta, Michigan, just north of Grand Rapids. Later, I ministered for them in another church in eastern Michigan and we became good friends along the way. In 2002, they joined us in Bicol as missionary associates. As a rule, missionary associates serve under career missionaries and many associates are only short term—two years or less. There is not necessarily the expectation that they will become missionaries for life. These days many do transition into becoming full-time missionaries.

Because we wanted them to give at least part of the time to assisting us, Deborah agreed to work in our home office twelve hours a week. She handled our financial reports, helped transcribe interviews for my dissertation and other things. The rest of the time they were free to pursue their own ministries. Ray was passionate about teaching and had a master's degree, so he was given the opportunity to teach in the Bible school. Prior to moving to Bicol, they had spent several months in Manila studying Tagalog. Ray had done quite well, despite the limited amount of time they were given. Since Tagalog was the language of instruction at EBC, Ray did his best to use Tagalog as much as he could.

Deborah's passion was children's ministry, especially in training children to minister to other children. She had over twenty years of experience in children's ministry before coming to the Philippines, and she was eager to engage in children's ministry there. She connected with the leadership of the district, and she did children's ministries' workshops all over the Bicol region. She did all this as well as serving as children's director of a local church in the Legaspi area. She and Ray also gave some supervision to the evangelistic team while we were in the States from April 2004 through May 2005.

They lived in the third-floor apartment on the roof of the Bible school. In anticipation of their arrival, we were given the opportunity to have a second STL car, something that was rarely done, and we made this car available to them to use. We enjoyed many times of fellowship with them, and they heartily participated in the BEEF group. We also greatly appreciated their contribution to the ministry. When they finished their commitment to Bicol, they transitioned into career missionaries and served in Mindoro, a mid-sized island southwest of Manila.

In reading this account, one might easily think that all we did was work, but this was not the case. I am an exercise nut and spent three to four hours a week either playing basketball or walking. Both of us are bookworms. Because I naturally read a lot of academic work in pursuing my dissertation, I normally opted for reading Christian fiction in the evenings and on our day off. I was a regular customer at a used book store in the mall in Legaspi. I also passed a good amount of time browsing the book stores in Manila whenever I could.

Since it was almost as cheap to eat out as it was to eat in our own kitchen, we spent many evenings in our favorite restaurants in Legaspi. Sometimes we were joined by missionary friends or Filipinos, but just the two of us often went out. Having our office in our home made it a bit challenging to separate ourselves from our work and eating out helped us to get away.

Several times a year we were also able to get away for a couple of days to seaside resorts that dotted the landscape outside of Legaspi. On a number of occasions, we were also able to spend a longer period at a resort about an hour south of Manila that had some wonderful amenities.

By the time April, 2004, rolled around we had finished the Tagalog *FLSB*, completed my dissertation, and concluded my term as the Country Moderator. By now, Alan had matured as a leader and was ready to lead the evangelistic team with occasional help from the Millers. Debbie had prepared the Bible school for her extended absence. It was time for us to return to the States for a year to visit our supporters (more than 100 churches all over America) and reconnect with family and friends for a year. We were ready for a change of scenery and a different, although challenging schedule.

CHAPTER 13

The Middle Years in Bicol
(2005-2009)

Our time in the States was uneventful. To date, it is the only itineration that we actually completed on time. We visited churches in a dozen states, travelling about 50,000 miles, mostly by driving. Keeping the old house in Daraga would have meant paying rent and utilities while we were gone, plus paying someone to live there and guard the house, so we gave it up when we went home. When we returned, the first order of business was to move into a new house that Deborah Miller had found for us. The new house was in the same subdivision as the old one, about six blocks away. This house had an open floor plan with no wall separating the kitchen and large living room, making it easier to host larger groups of people. Like the other house, this one also had a large room near the door that could be used for an office. Since I had a fairly large personal library, I took this space while Debbie used a smaller spare bedroom for her office, although she later moved into my office so we could see each other more often.

The owner had a beautiful garden in front of the house. This house had a much larger yard, so we decided to get a guard dog who would also be a pet. While in seminary I had a friend who had a Doberman that I really came to like, so I decided to get one. Dobermans are not indigenous to the Philippines, but we found a veterinarian who was able to get a male puppy for me, and I named him Sam. Thankfully he turned out to be part of a small sub-breed of Dobermans that was not violent towards people. Unfortunately, he did not like plants—especially the ones in the owner's garden—and proceeded to destroy the entire garden before we could stop him. He did not eat them. He just enjoyed destroying them. We ended up spending a lot of money to fence in the garden and replace the plants.

He was only about six weeks old when we got him. We had a good laugh when we discovered that while his body was quite small at the time, his paws were already fully grown, and it looked like he was walking on platforms! One morning Debbie heard him whining out in the carport where he lived. She looked out and discovered that he had his head butted against the stomach of a large tomcat. He did not want the cat there, but he had one problem. The cat was bigger and in no hurry to leave! That changed within about two months and the cats in the neighborhood correctly concluded that they were no longer welcome at our house!

As with the previous house, this house was completely walled in, with a pedestrian gate and a larger one for our car in the driveway. We bought Sam a large, hard plastic bench that served as his bed. Occasionally, I allowed him to run free in the neighborhood to get some exercise. If a neighbor's gate was open, Sam took the liberty to invite himself in to "visit." There was an open lot down the side where somebody kept a cow that Sam enjoyed tormenting. One day, however, when I tackled Sam in that lot to tie on his leash, the cow saw his opportunity to get revenge. He snuck up behind me and head-butted Sam in the stomach. Honestly, he deserved it. Thankfully, only his pride was hurt! I had to stop letting him go free when one of the neighbor kids complained that Sam was scaring the wits out of him. Taking him for a walk on a leash resolved these problems, but the other dogs on the street were never happy to see him.

I also taught him how to play "fetch" with a rubber ball, which I would usually throw against the wall of the carport for Sam to chase. In time, he became quite proficient at catching the ball as it came off the wall. The biggest part of the fun was that he did not want to give the ball back, so we had a tug-of-war with me pulling it out his mouth. A number of our Filipino friends were surprised to come by our house and see their missionary wrestling with his dog on the floor of the carport. I had many hours of fun with Sam and it was a great way to relax.

Alan had capably led the evangelistic team while we were gone, but I think he was glad to give the overall leadership back to me when we returned. Once we had gotten our household things out of storage at the Bible school and moved in, Debbie picked up her responsibilities again at EBC. I resumed traveling with the team, telling the greatest story ever told to thousands of Filipinos every month. I prayed with many of them to receive Christ. As before, my team and members of the church followed up as quickly and effectively as we could in order to conserve the fruit of the evangelistic rallies. We continued to give away New Testaments and Bibles that we purchased from The Bible League, who had a distributor right in Legaspi, whom Alan got to know pretty well. As before, we were happy to do rallies for either existing churches or for new church plants. That gave the Filipino pastors the opportunity to give guidance to our ministry and a share in the decision-making about where we would go.

Planting new churches is the greatest way to conserve the fruits of evangelism in any locale. Because Filipinos do not have the resources to travel far to go to church, it was imperative that we saturate the region with churches, even if they were small and unable to support a full-time pastor. While we continued to plant churches with the evangelistic team, I was also instrumental in bringing in a PGCAG-wide church planting program called Summer of Service (SOS).

Before we left for itineration in 2004, the district superintendent, Amberto Carilla, asked me to become the church planting director for the district, the first and only time I have ever taken an official position in the PGCAG leadership. Normally, this would be seen as a violation of indigenous church principles that called for PGCAG churches to be self-governing. I initially resisted his request, agreeing only after prayer and consultation with Bill Snider. I agreed because we also believed that true partnership means that the partners involved have the right to ask things of each other in a loving interdependent relationship. The indigenous church concepts, then, are flexible principles, not fixed laws.

In one respect I was not good at the job. Church planters need to be mentored. Since I had always been an evangelist and had never actually planted a church myself, it was hard for me to address practical issues of church planting despite my best efforts to do so. I have always tried to associate with people that have ministry gifts that I do not have, so I recruited a church-planting pastor to help me with this aspect. In the end, however, for whatever reason, one-on-one visits with church planters never did become a common feature of this job for me.

Where I did do well was in bringing in a national church-planting program called Summer of Service (SOS), mentioned above. This program called for recruiting young people, normally college age, to give one month of their summer vacation to help plant a church somewhere in the Philippines. The program began in 1986 under the leadership of Pastors Rey and Zenaida Calusay in their own church on the island of Panay. SOS ultimately spread all over the nation.

Since the program called for someone that had influence with the pastors, and the administrative skills needed for organizing a fairly sizable event, it was a much better fit for me. In 2006, I went to the Calusays' church for a week of training on how to lead a district-wide SOS program, and we began that year. I led the program for three years. I think we planted somewhere between seven and nine churches during that time, although a couple of them did not survive for various reasons.

From time to time, we also invited medical teams from the States to come and hold clinics, combining compassion ministry with evangelism and church planting. A normal clinic would consist of doctors, dentists, nurses, pharmacists and other medical professionals, as well as just ordinary people to help with the myriad of other tasks involved. We tapped local churches to provide spiritual counseling which was always a part of the program.

Normally people would be seen by a doctor or dentist before they would see a counselor. We had to change the plan for dental patients and have them go through counseling first. We discovered that people had a hard time talking to a counselor after having a tooth extracted! Since medical clinics could be used to gain entrance into communities for church planting purposes, I tried combining it with the SOS program. However, the SOS program is pretty structured and eventually we had to move the clinics to another time.

Since the clinics involved teams from the States, we always tried to include a bit of sightseeing and souvenir shopping while they were here. Two ladies from my home church in Grand Rapids came one year, and they wanted to ride a water buffalo, the most commonly used farm animal in the Philippines. While we were traveling back to Legaspi from a clinic one day, I saw a farmer walking along the road leading his water buffalo by rope. The water buffalo looked perfectly normal to my untrained eyes, but the farmer informed me that it could not be ridden because it was pregnant! Apparently animal husbandry was not my specialty. We eventually found a couple of water buffalo that could be ridden. While the American visitors were enjoying their rides, I had the opportunity to share Christ with one of the owners. In all, we hosted six teams over the years. While hosting them was not cheap and required a lot of work, it was another way to show the love of Christ to people, lead them to the Lord, and get them plugged into a local church. It also gave my evangelistic team a break from our normal evangelistic rallies, and I think they enjoyed working with the teams.

Medical teams were not the only teams we hosted. We hosted two teams from Southwestern Assemblies of God University (SAGU) in Waxahachie, Texas. At least two young ladies from these teams later became missionaries themselves. There were other teams as well. One of the most memorable was a team of women from Michigan. This team was headed by Mary Selzer, the director of Women's Ministries for the AG in Michigan. Mary and her husband, Lou, pastored a church in the Detroit area and were dear friends of ours.

On one of our itinerations, Debbie shared her burden with Mary for doing something for the women in ministry in the BRDCAG. Mary took the burden to heart. She organized a team of women from the churches in Michigan to come and minister to the needs of the women in BRDCAG through a special conference just for them. They also financed most of the expenses. Debbie organized the meeting on our end, which was to be held at a seaside resort about a half hour east of Legaspi. She recruited me to be her assistant, working in the background to make sure everything went okay. Normally, Alan would have also helped, but he had to stay home with their children so his wife could attend.

Excitement built as the time for the conference neared, but trouble also loomed. The resort was near the foot of Mt. Mayon and the mountain started to show signs of eruption. Most conventions were held at the Bible school, but Debbie wanted to give the BRDCAG ladies a treat by doing something different. When the mountain began to rumble, we began to reconsider this decision. In the end, Debbie and Mary decided to take the risk and hold the meeting at the resort, but we had a backup plan to move the conference to EBC in case the mountain erupted.

Many women came from a great distance by bus, and much to our dismay, some brought their husbands along, apparently mainly to protect their wives on the road. The problem was that the men also started to attend the sessions. Some of the Michigan ladies were not comfortable with this because they wanted to deal with sensitive women's issues. Some of the men were not happy when I told them they would have to leave. When they threatened to pack up their wives and go home, we reached a compromise. They could stay on the grounds but not attend the meetings. They agreed, apologies were exchanged on all sides and peace was restored. There was, however, one exception. One pastor from a nearby church brought his wife and wanted to stay. He was a fine fellow, but he did not pick up on our suggestions that he needed to leave. To make the point, I escorted him to the edge of the resort and gently but firmly tell him the day and time that he could return to pick up his wife. He took the news kindly and left, and we remained friends.

Even the mountain cooperated by not erupting, and the meeting went well. The Michigan ladies did a great job ministering to the Bicol ladies, who soaked it up like water on a dry sponge. They left feeling refreshed. We hosted a few other teams over the years, as well as numerous individual guests. These guests came to preach at the Bible study during our annual spiritual emphasis week, and to do seminars on leadership or the Holy Spirit, or other things. We also initiated, and hosted, a couple more conferences along with the BRDCAG leadership. All who came were a great blessing to the Filipinos and to us.

A couple of months before we returned from itineration in 2005, we received word that my successor as the country moderator, Dave Wenrich, and his family, were leaving the Philippines to serve elsewhere with AGWM. So, I was not too surprised when Bill Snider called a few weeks later and asked if I would be willing to assume the role again. After prayer, Debbie and I agreed. I served in this capacity again until our next itineration cycle in June 2009. The basic responsibilities had not changed, and as before, Bill gave me the freedom to be creative in this position.

This time, I had completed my doctorate and the Tagalog *FLSB* project. As a result, I invested more time in visiting missionaries in their various locations to stay updated on what they were doing, and what their concerns were. I also visited many of the twenty districts of the AG to listen and learn about how we might partner better with them in reaching Filipinos for Christ. At times, I spoke in their ministers' conventions. The entire PGCAG gathers every three years for a convention, business meetings, and elections. They usually ask an outsider to chair their elections, normally our area director. Since Bill and Kim were itinerating during the 2006 convention, I had the privilege of chairing the general superintendent's election that year.

During my first term as moderator, we conducted a field strategy review, which included input from the PGCAG leaders. In their written responses to our questionnaire, many noted that they needed help putting up church buildings. I did not think there was anything we could do on a national scale and I was ready to put the issue aside. Bill Snider had a different opinion and went to work on the matter. Missionaries in Africa had developed a program for making pre-fabricated church buildings in the States and shipping them in large containers to Africa. They had done quite well. Bill was able to get their construction plans, and he set to work to see if a similar program could be developed in the Philippines. He found that the construction plan had to be modified because of the climate differences. The Philippines experiences many typhoons, earthquakes, volcanic eruptions and other natural disasters every year, but apparently these do not happen as much in Africa.

He worked with architects and PGCAG leaders to lay the ground work. I was not involved much in the beginning, and I passed on my part to Dave Wenrich when he became the moderator. When I came back into the moderator's role, much work was done, some money was raised, and applications for buildings had been received from the PGCAG leaders. But no buildings had actually been put up. I was given the task of getting the project off the ground.

Never one to waste much time when given a task, I immediately contacted Rey Calusay, the assistant general superintendent of the PGCAG, and director of their home missions program. I asked him where I should begin. That resulted in a meeting at his church in Roxas City on the island of Panay in the western central part of the Philippines. It quickly became apparent that a number of issues still needed to be worked out before we could begin. It took a few months and another meeting or two to work out these issues, but we all worked hard and in the right spirit. I was joined in this effort by my missionary colleague,

Peg Lamb, who was working with the Calusays at the time. She served as the secretary for the project. Several staff members from Pastor Rey's church were also involved. Together, we made up the steering committee for this program with Pastor Rey as the chair.

We named this the *"Bayanihan* Program." *Bayanihan* is a Tagalog word that means working together to achieve a common goal. It is often caricatured by a picture of a dozen or so Filipino men carrying a small bamboo hut on poles to place it in a new location. The idea was that in working together in unity, we could achieve great things. When Pastor Rey became the general superintendent of the PGCAG at the election I chaired in 2006, he appointed my good friend, Johnny Vic Gallos, the district superintendent for the PGCAG churches in northern Panay and the islands associated with it, as his replacement. My job was to represent AGWM and be the liaison to churches in the States, which included fundraising—a bit to my dismay.

In 2006, new missionaries, Randle and Joyce Peterson, joined the committee. The Petersons had an extensive background in pastoring and church construction in the States before becoming missionaries. For health reasons, they remained based in the States and commuted back and forth to the Philippines. Randle's construction skills were badly needed and much appreciated. He worked well with an engineer named Tony, a member of Rey's church. Together they oversaw the bulk of the construction side of the project. Randle's home district in Louisiana made the *Bayanihan* Program their missions project one year. They raised funds for churches, and Randle took over my role as the main fundraiser. He did a much better job. He also brought a lot of teams from the States with him. He became the sole AGWM member of the committee when Peg and I moved on. Randall is still involved in the *Bayanihan* Program as of this writing. As of 2020, eighty-three churches have been built all over the islands.

Throughout this entire period, Debbie's work as president of the Bible school continued unabated. Students came, studied and graduated.

Many succeeded, but some did not, despite the faculty's best efforts to prepare them for ministry. Debbie needed help with some aspects of her job that she just could not stretch far enough to do, and she asked me to help. In the years following my resignation from the faculty, my role in the school had been minimal, and for the most part would continue to be. I attended major events, especially after Debbie became president. I invested a lot of money in maintaining the building, some of which called for my direct involvement. I worked together with the school business manager, Leonardo Orosco, and of course, Debbie.

In order to help Debbie, I asked for, and received, the title of Vice-President. I had no interest in adding another title to my resume, but I knew that the people I interacted with would ask what my position at the Bible school was. The title of "President's Husband" would not be sufficient for the job that needed to be done. This gave me the liberty for Debbie and me to pick and choose what I would do, given my limited time availability.

The specific job that needed to be done was to deal with two pieces of land that the school either owned or wanted to own. The school had formerly been located just outside of Iriga City, about ninety minutes' drive northeast of Legaspi. Two older faculty couples still lived on the property. The school had purchased the property back in the 1960s, but had never made the full payment. Consequently, while they had used the property ever since without complaint from the owners, they never had a clear title deed. Since the district wanted to retain the property, we were able to provide the funds for the purchase, and the deal was successfully completed.

The second piece of property was in Legaspi proper and had been purchased at the same time as the Daraga campus. However, it was later discovered that the property suffered major flooding during the rainy season. The school was neither able to build on it, nor despite our best attempts, able to sell it. When we left in 2013, the property still belonged to EBC.

I took the V.P.'s job with the understanding that I had no specific portfolio other than dealing with the real estate. I would also not be required to attend faculty meetings, partly because of my other workload. I did not realize until much later that this conveyed a message to Debbie that I was not all that interested in her work. While this was not true, actions do speak louder than words. In retrospect, I could have done better. The level of pain that my lack of support caused Debbie would not become apparent until a few years later.

While serving as the president of EBC, Debbie noted that the Bible schools were not turning out sufficient numbers of church planters to meet the staggering need to saturate the region with churches. She believed that the answer lay in training lay leaders to plant house churches all over the region. Because of the current responsibilities that I was already juggling, including those described in the next chapter, I simply could not participate in this project. Still, I certainly agreed that she could do it. In consultation with the Filipino church leadership, we determined that the best way to do this would be to provide training in multiple locations over a ten-month period. Considering that most of the lay people had jobs, we decided to limit the training to once a month, going all day on Friday, and Saturday until noon.

Debbie oversaw the program, but she enlisted others to do the actual training, since we had never planted a church ourselves. In this case, the church planters were trained to lead interactive Bible studies rather than preach. The thinking was that this might be a better way for individuals with no formal training in public speaking to disciple others. The training was also designed for the house church planting which would build into a church multiplication movement.

Our good friends in the BEEF group (see Chapter 11), Bob and Koleen French, had considerable experience in church planting and in training church planters. They eagerly accepted Debbie's invitation to do much of the training. They were well received by the PGCAG pastors.

Some of the PGCAG pastors who were experts in church planting were also invited to share in the training.

Over the course of two years, the training was done in ten different locations, and led to the planting of 206 churches. Since all of the laymen were members of AG churches, the house churches related to the church from which the leaders came in a mother/daughter relationship. This meant that the pastor of the mother church oversaw the house churches being planted by their members.

While all of this may have seemed to keep us busy enough, there was more to come.

CHAPTER 14

The Middle Years in Bicol
2005-2009 (Continued)

As I have already noted, the Bicol region was not immune to the natural disasters that often plague the Philippines. When typhoon Millennium hit in September 2006, I was in Singapore and Debbie was helping some new missionaries in Manila. This typhoon destroyed a lot of trees, but I do not recall that it did much else. Typhoon Reming, which hit us on November 30, 2006, was another story and we were home in Daraga when it happened.

Because we did not listen to much radio or TV, I did not even know the storm was coming until the morning it hit. We did manage to get out and buy some emergency supplies before the storm hit in force. For several hours, winds in excess of 120 m.p.h./250 k.p.h. pummeled our region, making the rain fly sideways at a ninety-degree angle—something I have never seen before or since. Like most houses in the Philippines, our house was not well insulated, and rain came in through every pore in the wall or roof—it was hard to tell which. We started mopping up excess water about noon and did not stop until 10 p.m. Even then, we did not get all the water out of the house. The power company knew the storm was coming and wisely turned off the power before it hit. Even Sam had to try to find a place to hide and was not entirely successful. We tried bringing him inside and locking him in a bathroom. He did not appreciate this and barked until we let him go back to the carport. The floor in my office was slightly elevated and somehow, and it had no pores in the walls or ceiling. It was the only dry place in the house. We pulled the mattress off our bed and slept on the floor of the office.

All phone service, cell and landline, was knocked out, as was the water. Early the next morning, we were awakened by Bible school students pounding on our gate to see if we were okay. We invited them in. There was meat in the freezer and the freezer could not run because we had no electricity. Debbie cooked it and we fed the students breakfast after they cleaned up what water remained on our floor. Fortunately, the house sustained only minor damage to the roof, and the landlord had it fixed as soon as he could.

The students shared what had happened at EBC during the typhoon. The school was on high ground so they were safe, but those living in the valley behind the back wall of the school had a different experience. The creek running through the valley had become a raging river. The locals scaled trees or got on their roofs to avoid being swept away in a flash flood. The students saw what was happening, and offered them shelter if they could climb over the wall. About 350 did so.

The most immediate problem we had to deal with, aside from cleaning our own house up, was how to feed our unexpected guests. The roads were littered with downed electrical and telephone wires, trees that the previous typhoon did not destroy, and parts of people's houses. One student and I drove all over town to find a couple of 50kg (110lbs) bags of rice, which would only feed these people for a couple of days. I think we also found some vegetables. It was a miracle we did not get a flat tire because there were probably a lot of nails and other sharp objects among the debris.

After a couple of days, the government was able to start providing food, but the people continued to stay at the Bible school because there was no place else to go. When the water receded after the typhoon, they discovered that the water had brought down soil from nearby Mt. Mayon. Most of the homes were completely or partly covered, making them unlivable.

For about a month, we could not hold any classes because the classrooms were full of people. To their credit, the students willingly gave of themselves to serve the guests with whatever they needed. The students learned lessons about servanthood which we could never have taught them in the classroom. Most of the guests were kind, but some of them helped themselves to the students' clothing, including their undergarments! When the AGWM sent us some disaster relief funds to help, part of the funds went to buying replacements for our students.

The morning of the typhoon, a neighbor came and asked if he could pump water from the manual pump in our backyard. He inadvertently became an answer to prayer. He was a plumber and when I told him it was broken, he replied, "I'll fix it." Five minutes later, he had water gushing out of the pump. Knowing that nobody had any water, we decided to tie Sam up, open the gate and invite the neighbors to use our pump. And they did. They came with their pails every day for at least three weeks, until the city could fix the pipes damaged by the typhoon. They not only carried water home, they also did their laundry and took baths right at our pump. Debbie and I had been praying for a way to minister to our neighbors, but I have to confess that this is not what we had in mind. We hired a guard to make sure that everything in our yard stayed there. We also told him to help older ladies carry their water home. He did, and shared the gospel with them on the way! Debbie also hung the words of Isaiah 12:3 in our carport, "With joy you shall draw water from the wells of salvation" (ESV).

Tens of thousands of homes were damaged or destroyed, including the home of one of Debbie's maids, Analyn Abinion, and her husband, Noel. Since we had a guest room, they moved in and stayed . . . for two and a half years! Their first daughter was later born while they were with us and she brought great joy to us all. They were a great help around the house and we loved them dearly.

With Noel and Analyn taking care of the house, and Alan and the team involved with various aspects of disaster relief, Debbie and I were able to keep a pre-planned commitment to spend Christmas in the States. We had only planned to be gone a couple of weeks, but Debbie got sick. I returned on schedule to help with the pressing needs of recovery from the typhoon, but Debbie spent an additional two weeks with her family. She enjoyed being pampered by her mother, a retired nurse.

All in all, AGWM put about $90,000 of relief funds in our hands, including $40,000 that was designated for food. By this time, dozens of relief agencies from all over the world had come to lend a hand, including CBN's Operation Blessing, which set up camp at our Bible school for a time. Convoy of Hope, with whom AGWM has a strong relationship, also came. I met with the BRDCAG leaders to determine how to use the given funds. We wanted to make sure that we met real needs and did not overlap with what other agencies were doing.

We used the $40,000 for food as designated, and bought 623 bags of rice and other food, some of it donated by Convoy of Hope. These meant that each church got only a few bags to share with their members, but it helped meet a need. In some cases, our neighbors were refused government aid because they were not Catholic. The Philippine constitution does guarantee freedom of religion, but it was difficult to enforce in all local situations. Because some of the food went to the pastors of each church, we encouraged the members to give some of their share to their neighbors instead of their pastor, as a way of expressing Christ's love. Many did so.

Many members' homes were damaged, or even lost entirely, on a scale that was beyond our ability to help. Yet, we were able to use some of the funds to help rebuild the fifty-four PGCAG churches in the region that had been damaged or destroyed. Thankfully, other organizations with more resources were able to help with rebuilding. We then used the remaining funds to start some livelihood projects to help our pastors into the future. Unfortunately, for one reason or another, none of the projects survived long term.

Tens of thousands of Bicolanos, like our neighbors at EBC, were left homeless and had to be sheltered in schools. The schools were used as evacuation centers until the homes could be repaired or rebuilt. Once we had our relief projects set in motion, we were able to do some evangelistic outreaches in some of these centers. The greatest tragedy of typhoon Reming was that it caused two major mudslides of Mt. Mayon, instantly killing around 2,000 people. At one of our outreaches, Debbie met a lady who lost several children, and twelve grandchildren, in one of these slides. We could not even imagine her heartache! I am thankful that whether in our evangelistic outreaches or through our relief efforts, our greatest offer was eternal hope in Jesus Christ.

Most Bicolanos were staunchly Catholic, although the majority were only nominally so. They were somewhat resistant to evangelicals. Since many of the relief agencies were evangelical and because their efforts covered many needs throughout the entire region, we noticed that there was a different attitude towards us in the months that followed the typhoon. Many people came to really know the Lord and were added to our churches. Debbie and I were thankful to God that we had been able to go through this experience with people we loved. Also, we were filled with gratitude to serve them in their hour of need to the best of our ability, thanks to the backing of the AGWM and many of our supporters in America. After about three months, with long term recovery still underway, we were able to resume our normal lives and schedules.

During my first term as country moderator, I began to ask myself some questions that any leader needs to ask. First, as I looked around at the various Bible schools and churches, etc., that had been started by previous generations of missionaries, I began to ask myself, "Why did they do what they did?" My missiological training at AGTS had pointed me towards some of the answers. But understanding what my predecessors had done, when and why they did what they did, remained unanswered. Then, I found myself asking another question: "Who were my predecessors?" While I knew, or had heard about some of them, for the most part, I did not have a clue.

At the same time, Debbie, too, began to get the feeling that this was a story that needed to be told. After prayer, much thought and consultation with Bill Snider, we concluded that God was leading me to research and write the story. By this time, we were home on itineration (2004-2005), and we decided to collect what data we could from the home office. While on our "pilgrimage" to the AGWM headquarters in Springfield, MO, to participate in the School of Missions, we added a day or two to the schedule. We made an appointment to visit the AGWM archives, which was headed by a delightful lady named Gloria Robinett.

We had no idea what we were getting into. It was not until we began to dig into Gloria's files that we began to realize how big this project was going to be. From the time of the first missionaries' arrival in Manila in 1926, until the time of the book's publishing in 2009, at least 302 AGWM missionaries had served in the Philippines. We quickly realized that we could not possibly review and xerox all of the newsletters, letters, faxes, field notes and many other things that we found in the files in the short time we had to spend there. Gloria graciously offered to do it for us, and over the next few months, she sent several boxes of documents to us in Michigan. Since itineration was an all-consuming task that left little time for anything else except reading, we had to wait until we returned to the Philippines to begin work on the project. We shipped the research files along with everything else we took back with us to Legaspi.

Once we settled back in Legaspi and received all of the goods that we had shipped, I began reading through the reams of data, marking the things that I thought were important to the story. As he had done with my dissertation, Alan served as my research assistant. I also received help from the other team members, who copied the things I marked onto four by six-inch index cards. Then, they categorized and filed the index cards. I never counted the cards, but the stacks continued to grow, and grow, as we went along. Like I had done with my past research projects, I did this as we traveled to our evangelistic rallies and when I traveled for my country moderator responsibilities. By this time, my wife and my team members had long become used to seeing me with my head buried in research while we traveled, while staying in homes or churches, and even at outreach sites, when I was not preaching. They gladly took up the other ministry duties to give me the time I needed.

Historians have to answer six basic questions. Who did the work, what did they do, as well as how, when, where and why did they do it? While I was not a professionally trained historian, I have read history voraciously for decades. I felt I could tell the missionaries' stories and answer these questions as well as anybody.

From the beginning, I determined to tell a balanced story that included the good, the bad and the ugly, that neither lionized nor libeled anyone. I am convinced that the reason that biblical writers described the good and the bad in the biblical characters was so only God would be glorified. As Paul wrote, we have this treasure (the gospel) in earthen vessels, which is us. We all are deeply flawed, in order that people may see Jesus Christ, not just us. (II Cor. 4:7 KJV)

While reviewing the research that Gloria had sent, I was also able to uncover other sources of research, which made our files even larger. After about fifteen months of researching and copying, I was finally able to begin writing a rough draft in September 2006. As I wrote, many gaps in the research became apparent, which called for contacting as many of the former missionaries as I could find.

The challenge is that much of the research I had were missionaries' newsletters. For fear of being misunderstood, and possibly losing support, most reported only the victories, which is hardly a balanced view of missionary life. If problems were discussed at all, they were usually mentioned as generic, or even "unspoken," prayer requests. This meant further digging to uncover these stories. Somehow, we managed to cobble together a list of contact information for many of the former missionaries. We carried on extensive correspondence, getting more answers to the questions of what they had done, etc., which were truly illuminating. Many were willing to admit to their struggles and gave me permission to publish their stories.

One missionary wrote that he had dealt with depression and suicidal thoughts. As I was writing his story into the larger narrative of the book, memories of my mother's depression and suicide attempts surfaced in my mind. Without warning, I experienced an eruption of private pain. I started to sob like someone who had just lost a loved one. Debbie, who by now had moved her desk into my office, immediately rushed over and threw her arms around my neck, asking me what was wrong. For several minutes, I was sobbing so hard that I could not answer. When I stopped crying, I was able to explain to her that this missionary's story had brought up the pain of the past. Beyond that, even I had no idea why I had reacted so strongly. At that time, I had no idea how much pain from my past lay buried in the recesses of my heart and mind. The missionary later complimented me on how well I told his story, having no idea how well I understood at least part of his pain. Even I had no clue as to how much better I would relate to him later. That story is told in the next chapter.

Other stories were simply hilarious, and I found a way to include many of them as well. Since I wanted to title the book, *Led by the Spirit*, Debbie challenged me that I needed to be able to prove that the missionaries were, in fact, led by the Spirit of God, not simply their own convictions or ego. I asked every missionary to tell me how they came to know Christ, how they were subsequently baptized in the Holy Spirit according to Acts 2:4. I further asked them how the Lord led them to the Philippines and in their ministries when they were there. I was amazed by their responses.

We were determined to tell the missionaries' stories as part of the grand metanarrative of what God was doing. This required doing it in chronological order. Within each period, however, we had to weave back and forth to include each story. We included the ministry in which the missionaries were working, such as Bible schools, orphanages, etc. Careful editing was required to stitch all the stories together. Neither Debbie nor I recall ever reading a book where the stories of so many people were told!

Any author rewrites the manuscript many times, and I was no exception, especially as new information continued to be discovered. The publisher, ICI Ministries in Manila, required that the manuscript be edited by at least two editors. They approved Debbie as one, since they knew about her background in English. The other was Donna Swinford, a professional editor that worked in the Church School literature department at the AG headquarters in Springfield. Additionally, Donna worked as a free-lance editor on the side. Working with an editor 8,000 miles away, and across fourteen times zones, had its challenges, but Donna was superb and did a great job for us, as did Debbie. Both made the text much more readable and enjoyable. It was a delight to work with them.

That being said, however, the editing and rewriting a manuscript of nearly 700 pages was a lot of work. In order to publish it in time for the PGCAG General Council in April 2009, we really had to work hard. Not only did I do it, often until 10 p.m. on many, many nights, but I pushed Debbie to do the same, causing tension in our marriage. While she picked up on this right away, I did not do so until much later. The consequences of my action, and the price we paid for it, will be further explained in the next chapter.

Because Bill Snider knew that I would want to write a balanced view of our history, including the bad along with the good, he approved the project on the condition that I submit the manuscript to a committee of missionaries that he would appoint and chair. Bill's intent was not to squelch what I would say, but to make sure that I did not say anything unnecessarily offensive. He appointed Paul Klahr, a retired missionary that had served in the Philippines in the 1970s and 1980s, John Carter, to work with him. I had only met Paul Klahr once in passing, but John had been involved with my MA thesis and doctoral dissertation. He was a real blessing then, and he would be in this project as well. Everyone was easy to work with, and the objections they raised were minor and easily corrected. In fact, the only change Paul requested was that I spell his name correctly. In one reference, I referred to him as "Paula" instead of "Paul!" John Carter, on the other hand, was quite thorough by nature. He went well above and beyond the call of duty. He marked every grammatical and punctuation error that he saw that had somehow slipped by the editors and me. He really helped improve the manuscript!

Finally, we sent the book off to the publisher. Angel Mendoza, who works for ICI, did a great job on the layout. The book cover was designed by Mil Santos, who had also designed the cover of the Tagalog *FLSB*, and with whom we would develop a long-term working relationship and personal friendship. I had no idea then, what a critical role she would fill for me when we moved to APTS a few years later.

We printed 3,000 copies of the book. I immediately shipped 1,000 copies to the States to sell and to give to our supporters during our upcoming itineration. ICI Ministries, who also handled the marketing in the Philippines in the beginning, brought 100 copies to the PGCAG General Council meeting. The general superintendent gave me a few moments in an afternoon session to promote the book, and ICI sold every copy they brought.

The book sold reasonably well on itineration. The former missionaries were so excited about their stories being put in print that they were anxiously waiting for it to come out. They bought copies as soon as they could. At least a couple of former missionaries bought multiple copies. When we returned from itineration, however, ICI informed me that the book had not sold well in the Philippines.

Discounting the price resolved the problem, and over the next several years we sold out the entire stock in the country.[1]

Looking back, the book achieved its purposes. I most certainly found the answers to the questions that I was asking. The book also provided a way for other missionaries to learn their history without having to do all the research. The endnotes documenting my research also left a trail that other researchers could follow. I am aware of at least one Bible school teacher who used it as a textbook in his Philippine church history class.

The overall feedback I received on the book was good. Several students have used it in writing their research papers, and at least four scholars have referenced it in their thesis or dissertation. As with any other author, however, there were a few detractors. One Filipino family, whose father had been a part of one of the major problems dealt with in the book, actually threatened to sue me for libel, although they presented no evidence that what I said was inaccurate. Thankfully, the threat never materialized.

In the middle of writing *Led by the Spirit,* another opportunity came our way rather unexpectedly. One day my wife ran into Edgar (Egay) Ebojo, a friend of ours who worked at the Philippine Bible Society (PBS). Egay mentioned that perhaps we should consider doing the *FLSB* in Cebuano, the dominant language of part of the central islands, as well as Mindanao, the large island in the south. There had been a call for this from some of the PGCAG leaders in the past, but we were not able to act on it at that time. In this case, Debbie did not realize that Egay was only joking, and Egay did not know that Debbie took him seriously. Debbie was excited about the possibility when she relayed his suggestion to me. I began to seriously think about how this might be done.

When PBS saw that we were serious about it, they decided to get onboard. Life Publishers, AGWM and the PGCAG also supported the

---

[1]The book is still available in pdf form from me and I can be reached at dave.johnson@agmd.org or it can be downloaded free from my account at www.academia.edu.

idea. This time, however, we needed to do things differently. The most logical place to base the project was Cebu City, one of the largest cities in the country, located in the center of the Philippines. At that time, there were only a couple of flights a day from Legaspi, and they all went only to Manila. There were a couple of months a year when one airline company or another would have a direct flight to Cebu City a few days a week, and even then, they did not fly consistently. Also, the flights to Manila often did not have a connecting flight to Cebu until the next day, meaning that I would consume a lot of time just in commuting if I was going to handle the project directly.

Fortunately, PBS was willing to handle the project, with minimal oversight from me. This called for a redefinition of my role as the managing editor. Instead of managing the translators and editors, I became responsible for establishing and maintaining the partnership between PBS, Life Publishers, the AGMF and the PGCAG. In essence, I represented all of the others to PBS and vice versa.

The glue that held the whole partnership together was a carefully outlined memorandum of agreement that spelled out the conditions, duties and line of authority for all parties. The PGCAG agreed to the partnership arrangement on the condition that all translators and editors be baptized in the Holy Spirit with the evidence of speaking in other tongues, the traditional AG position. PBS, on the other hand was an ecumenical organization, with representatives on their board from various Christian traditions, including some Catholic bishops and the PGCAG general superintendent, Rey Calusay. For the PBS top leadership, the condition set by the PGCAG was no problem, especially since the General Secretary of the PBS, Nora Lucero, was a PGCAG pastor's wife. However, they were concerned that this might be a problem for their ecumenically oriented board, who had to approve the memorandum. One of the PBS leaders suggested that we could resolve the issue by stating in the memorandum that the AGMF would have the final decision on who would be approved as a translator or editor. This suggestion worked brilliantly. I worked with PBS to recruit PGCAG pastors to serve as translators and editors, and PBS provided the training and project oversight.

The project finally got off the ground in 2008. Once it was up and running, my role became minimal. I made sure that PBS and Life maintained good communications and intervened to help solve any problems as they occurred. With my small role, Life and PBS were able to carry on the project even while Debbie and I were home for itineration. I interacted by email as needed.

As our third missionary term came to a close in 2009, we had spent nine years in Bicol. Much had been accomplished and we were grateful. We had succeeded in most of what we had done. By this time, Alan had matured to the point that he could lead the team without supervision, although we kept in contact through email.

On the outside we looked great. I had finished the book and completed two more two-year terms as the country moderator. We conducted another 200 or more outreaches, planting new churches and helping existing ones. Debbie had completed her second three-year term as president of EBC and declined reappointment. She had also launched the church planting schools and was highly regarded by all who knew her. We had participated in a major disaster relief effort and had successfully hosted a number of teams.

But on the inside, things were different. As we packed up our belongings for storage at EBC, sent our dog to live with some missionary friends while we were gone, and said goodbye to our friends and co-workers, I had this gnawing feeling that we would be gone longer than the anticipated year or so, although I did not know why. While there had been hints along the way, neither of us saw the emotional and mental tsunami that was about to hit us.

CHAPTER 15

Depression, Burnout, and Healing

I t all started with a heated argument between Debbie and me. An argument that lasted four hours. Debbie had been telling me for the last year or so that we needed to get some marriage counseling, but I thought otherwise. I was in denial, and my denial could have cost us dearly. By this time, we had been in the States for a few weeks. We were in Springfield, Missouri, for the annual AGWM School of Missions for itinerating missionaries. There we learned that one of AGWM's counseling ministries, Missionary Renewal Asia Pacific (MRAP), now known primarily as Ministry Resources International (MRI), would be hosting a seminar on training pastoral counselors. Debbie wanted to stay, thinking it would help us with our own issues. Since I was in denial, I disagreed and the verbal battle ensued.

In the end, we could not stay because we had purchased a car once we got home to Michigan. We had a temporary license plate that would expire shortly after we returned from Missouri. If we had stayed, we would have driven home illegally on expired license plates. But the real reason we did not stay for the training was my own stubbornness. The one positive outcome of the argument is that I came to the conclusion that Debbie was right. We needed help.

The ensuing two months clearly revealed how desperate we were. Debbie began showing signs of burnout. I became even more alarmed when I began to be barraged with the temptation to commit suicide. Debbie became petrified that I might harm myself. At that point, I had no idea why these thoughts were coming and I did not know how to control, or get rid of, them. These thoughts would constantly torment me for at least the next fourteen months. I contacted Dr. Jack Rozell, the director of MRAP, in Kirkland, Washington, just east of Seattle. He gave me his personal cell phone number. He told me to call him anytime, day or night, if I needed him. I called many times.

In early September, we flew to Seattle for a week of evaluation at the MRAP offices. There, we determined that we needed to stop itineration and come to MRAP for at least three months. That three months became one year. The AGWM leadership, and our supporting churches, were behind us all the way. They never hesitated to give us the time we needed to be away from our work, fully aware that we might never return to the Philippines.

Since MRAP did not have any openings for about three weeks, we went home and I resumed itineration, including a nine-day blitz of churches in New England, which I did alone. At one point, I had lunch with the pastor of a supporting church. Since he had become the pastor during our last term in the Philippines, I had never met him before. While sitting in a restaurant discussing our work, an emotional dam inside me broke and without warning, I started sobbing like a child. I poured out my whole story, including my thoughts of suicide. This man was a godly, veteran pastor and he spent the next hour or two just listening and pouring healing balm on my troubled soul. After this, I could hardly wait to stop traveling and get to MRAP.

We arrived back at MRAP around the end of September. MRAP was founded in 1995 by Jack and Adel Rozell, who were missionaries at APTS. They had had to return home suddenly when Adele became ill and could not continue to serve in Asia. She and Jack, who had already been a pastoral counselor for many years before going to APTS, felt led by the Lord to start a ministry to help missionaries in crisis.

MRAP had a lease on a house in Everett, WA, about a thirty-minute drive north of their offices, where Debbie and I stayed for the first seven months. When they lost the lease, we moved to a long term stay hotel in Bothell, just south of Everett along the freeway going to Kirkland, for another four and a half months. We found Everett to be a quiet, peaceful community with a really nice YMCA[1] where we could get our exercise. By God's grace, Debbie's hometown, Bellevue, WA, where her parents still lived, was about thirty minutes south of Kirkland, or about an hour from Everett. Three of Debbie's four brothers and their families lived within an hour's drive of Bellevue.

As we settled in, we needed to find a church to attend. Since we were on leave from AGWM to pursue healing, we did not want to do any ministry, but we wanted to at least be able to attend Sunday services. The Neighborhood Church in Bellevue, Debbie's home church, was too far for us to attend regularly. We checked out a couple of churches in the Everett area, including a fairly large church once pastored by Debbie's grandfather. Then, we discovered that Debbie's former youth pastors, Steve and Debbie Alsup—who had also been missionaries—were pastoring in the area.

When Debbie contacted Steve, he mentioned that it was actually a house church that met in a recreation room in a senior's living facility in Bothell. There were eight people, including us, the first Sunday we were there. Rather than a traditional church service with music and a message by the pastor, this group was focused on prayer and discussion of biblical concepts, often using a book by a Christian author as a study guide. When they all introduced themselves in the first service we attended, one of the men said ". . . and as we get comfortable with one another, we open up and share our hurts and our pain." We had found a church home, and the people who attended quickly became friends. For the next year, we poured out a lot of pain, and they offered us listening ears and loving hearts. We tried to do the same for them.

One of our struggles, especially for Debbie, was that her mother had been diagnosed with Alzheimer's, which is a slow, cruel, terminal disease

---

[1] Young Men's Christian Association.

that affects the mind. There is no known cure. By the time we arrived in 2009, she was already losing her memory, especially the names of some of her five children, and all of her eleven grandchildren. She almost always recognized us at this point, although on one occasion she asked if we were her parents. This was really hard for Debbie and her family. Still, the opportunity to spend a lot of good quality time with them over the course of a year helped Debbie deal with her grief.

I think Alzheimer's may be harder for the family than it is for the victim. The victims live in the moment because they cannot remember the past, whether good or bad, unless someone reminds them. They also tend to lack awareness of how their disease impacts their family and friends. We had heard that some Alzheimer's patients get violent, but fortunately, this was not the case with Debbie's mom, although she was prone to wander. We often took her to the mall to get some exercise and spend time with her. Debbie was as attentive to her mother as anyone could be, but one day, while I was visiting a coffee shop, they were strolling through a department store. Debbie turned to look at something for just a moment and her mom wandered off. Debbie was frantic with worry when she called me. We eventually found Mom sitting on a park bench just outside the mall. She was fine, but was totally unaware of what she had done.

We went to counseling for about two hours a day, four days a week. Jack and his team decided that they would deal with our individual issues first, and as we began to work through them, then they would give us marriage counseling. We were happy with that plan. There were also books to read, and videos to watch, that also contributed to our healing process.

God was at the center of the whole process, from beginning to end. In the beginning, I usually met with either Jack or Larry Steller, one of the other members of the team with a lot of pastoral experience. Debbie usually met with either Jack or Sallee Conn, who with her husband Jim, had been missionaries in Tonga and were now serving at MRAP. Sallee soon became Debbie's confidant and close friend. Jim led a men's group with discussion sessions that met for a couple of months. He had other responsibilities as well.

MRAP also had a relationship with a Christian psychiatrist, who had a private practice nearby. I ended up seeing him at least twice a month. When he formally diagnosed me as being severely depressed, I broke down in his office and cried like a baby. I was gripped by the fear that I was going the same route as my mother, including medication and admittance to mental wards in hospitals. He did put me on medication, which I have continued to take since that time. Jack assured me that there had been great advances in psychiatric treatment, and that hospitals would not be necessary. Thankfully, he was right. But he also told me that while the medications would help "calm the waters" of depression, they did not deal with the root causes. This would have to be done by the Holy Spirit, the counseling team, and me. As we dug deeper into the issues, we discovered that some of them were deeply rooted in the past. I learned I had been more deeply impacted by my mother's issues than I had ever realized.

From the time that my mother began having mental problems when I was only eleven years old, my brothers and I could never depend on her being there when we needed her. This left me profoundly scarred, with feelings of abandonment. On at least four occasions, she had attempted suicide through overdosing on prescription medication. On one of those occasions, when I was about fourteen, I was the one who discovered her comatose body (see chapter 2). This impacted me more severely than I could have known at the time.

Out of this situation, and without knowing it, I developed a defense mechanism of trying to control my world, and the people closest to me, especially Debbie. Along with this came anger issues. We had known for a long time that I had a problem controlling my anger, but neither Debbie nor I understood the source of my anger until then.

I always thought that the Holy Spirit was a gentleman, but some of these Spirit-directed counseling sessions were brutal. I wept on many occasions. God is always loving, but sometimes love has to be tough. Facing the issues was really hard. By this time, I was fifty-two years old, meaning that some of these issues had been in my heart and soul for over forty years. Dealing with them took time, a lot of hard work, and lots of emotional energy.

For the first few months, our healing was delayed because we were both physically exhausted from our labors on the field, especially from the last two years during the final push to get my book finished. When I realized what I had done to both Debbie and myself, I had to accept responsibility for what I had done to her and apologize.

I came to feel that I was responsible for our need to take a year away from our ministry. One Sunday afternoon when we had been there about four months, I was having an emotional pity party and blaming myself for everything that had gone wrong. Then God spoke to me as clearly as I have ever heard his voice. He said "David, you are here because I love you and I have set you aside in order that I might heal you." In other words, while I was responsible for my workaholic attitude, anger, and a number of other things, God was ultimately the one responsible for us going to MRAP, not me. Looking back, I think that was a turning point in my healing journey. Knowing that my suffering had purpose made it a bit easier to bear.

A big part of the journey was dealing with a negative self-image that contributed to my suicidal thinking. Jack taught me the acronym called "the KRY method:" *Know* who I am in Christ; *Reckon* myself dead to sin and negative, suicidal thinking; *Yield* myself to Christ and his love, not to the flesh. Jack and Larry also taught me how to face my pain by drawing the analogy of Jesus in Gethsemane. Jesus had a choice. He could face the pain and shame of bearing our sin on the cross, or he could call for angels in heaven to deliver him. He chose the pain, knowing that the results would literally be out of this world!

I had the choice to either face my pain, or follow the lie that suicide was a good way out. Facing my pain was the hardest thing I have ever done, but I chose to face my pain, take responsibility for the mistakes that I made, and grow. I had to make that choice every single day for months and still have to do so, although not as often. My experience is that issues that came all the way from my childhood need time to heal.

Another step in healing my suicidal thinking was to consider who I would hurt if I were to take my life. It would devastate Debbie, our families, and hurt my many friends all over the world, as well as the thousands we had ministered to over the years. More than anything else, it would be an insult to the one who faced his pain, died, and rose again to take my pain away. Since I did not want to hurt anyone, thinking about this helped me to step away from the brink of disaster.

Dealing with my own issues helped me deal with the way I saw my mother's issues. For years, I had questioned how a wonderful, otherwise godly woman, who loved God and family with all of her heart, could even think of attempting suicide. I had to admit that I did not know, and concluded that I had to leave the matter with God. During our counseling, I think it was Larry who suggested that perhaps my mom did not see any other way to escape her pain. I think he had a valid point. In dealing with my own crisis, I came to realize that this was entirely possible, although I still have to leave the ultimate answer in the hands of God. He might explain it to me someday in heaven, but by that time, it will not matter anymore.

In many ways, my mother was a wonderful example of love and godliness to me. But like anyone else, she was human. I had to realize that she did not set a good example by attempting to take her own life, and I had to learn to forgive her. In helping me with this, my counselors repeatedly stated that they had no desire to disparage my memories of my mother. But I did have to face the fact that my past was not as pristine as I had once thought. I could excuse the depression as not being her fault, but her suicide attempts were not accidental. I had to forgive Mom for being a poor example of how to deal with emotional pain. It was a hard lesson to learn, but I have discovered that the truth is liberating (John 8:32). I had to revise my view of my mother, but it never lessened my love for her, and I am absolutely convinced that she is with Jesus in heaven today. Like me, she was forgiven by grace. Thank God that worthiness is not required. With this, and many other issues, I had to recognize that while I could not change the past, I could change my perspective of it. And, with God and my counselors' help, I did. Looking at the past now still brings some regret about the things that happened, but the pain is mostly gone.

While I was not consciously aware of this, one way I had coped with my feelings of abandonment, which included an irrational fear of boredom, was to overwork. While all of the projects I had been involved in were good, and to this day, I believe that God was in them. I now recognize that part of my motivation for working so hard was the fear of being bored. In this respect, not all of my reasons for working were righteous, and I had to repent not only to God, but also to my wife. Debbie and I both had to learn to have more balance in life and limit the number of hours that we worked. For years, sixty-hour workweeks, with all of the attendant stresses on ourselves and our marriage, were normal. Since then, we have cut our normal workweek to about forty to forty-five hours, with some exceptions. We now have many more quiet evenings at home, which I really look forward to at the end of the day. And I am not bored!

Like any preacher or author, I went through dry spells in not knowing what to preach and write, etc., although I have always had good study habits. Some of these spells were long. Once we began to get more balance in life, my mind was refreshed, and now I have more ideas about what to preach and write than I have time in which to do them. A healthier lifestyle has greatly increased my creativity, and I am now a liberated workaholic!

Meanwhile, Debbie was dealing with burnout, her mother's situation, and many other issues. Most of it is not my story to tell. Like me, she began to slowly heal. On several occasions Jack and others shared with us that the healing journey was not a straight line. It was full of backtracking and moving forward again. Also, we began to see that dealing with our pain was somewhat like peeling an onion. There were multiple levels of our pain, and the Holy Spirit normally dealt with one level at a time. The Word of God, like a surgeon's scalpel, cut deeply, and it hurt, but the purpose was to heal, not harm (Heb. 4:12). And, also, like cutting an onion, there were a lot of tears!

There's a lot of truth to the statement that hurting people hurt others. Because of our own issues, Debbie and I had deeply hurt one another. After about eight or nine months of primarily focusing on our individual issues, we were well enough to begin confronting our marital issues. In a number of ways, I was far from being an ideal husband.

As I mentioned earlier, Debbie was absolutely petrified by my suicidal thoughts, and for a while, was afraid to leave me alone. She was also deeply hurt by my anger, especially since she bore the brunt of it for many years, although I was never physically abusive. The number of examples that could be given would probably fill an entire book. She also felt that I had not adequately supported her work at EBC, and I had to admit that she was right. On many occasions over the years, we both spoke in chapel. While she was normally there whenever I spoke, I cannot remember a single time that I was present when she spoke. I normally used the excuse that I was too busy with my own work. Little did I recognize how utterly selfish I was.

Furthermore, since I grew up in a home with a stay-at-home mother who took care of most of the housework, I expected the same from Debbie, despite her full-time ministry load. To my way of thinking, the kitchen was only for eating, and I left nearly all of the cooking and dishwashing to her. We also enjoy a cup tea in the evening. Seldom did I offer to serve her. In these and several other ways, I had failed to love

Debbie in the same, sacrificial manner that Christ loved the Church (Eph. 5:28).

We also had communication issues. Like most men, my need to talk and listen is much less than Debbie's. The fact that we were both bookworms did not help in this case. I had some issues to overcome.

In sum, I spent a lot of time that year repenting before God and Debbie. But talk is cheap. Saying that I was sorry was much easier than actually changing—but words without action are worthless. By God's grace, Debbie's patience, and my counselors' willingness to confront me in love with all of my shortcomings, my attitude and actions began to change. When that happened, and when Debbie began to confront the ways in which she had hurt me, our marriage began to heal. I am still far from perfect, but I now make sure I am there as much as possible whenever she preaches. I willingly wash dishes (normally without complaining) and share the tea serving duties at night. We engage in good conversation somewhere along the way—although I am still working on this one. Debbie is a lot happier and so am I.

By the September 2010, we had been at MRAP for a year. While we were still working through some issues, my depression was much better. My suicidal thoughts were greatly lessened and gradually became a thing of the past. Yet, I still battle depression and continue to take medication for it daily, but the severity of the depression has greatly lessened. Over the year, God had also healed Debbie of burnout and other things. With our bodies, souls and spirits renewed, we were ready to resume itineration with different attitudes and a more balanced lifestyle. We had been healed of much, but if one were to look close enough, one can still see that we are a work still in process.

There are no words to express how grateful to God I am for what he has done. But God was not the only one we needed to thank. Without Jack and the whole MRAP team, and without the full support of our AGWM leadership, as well as the unswerving support of our families, friends (especially those in the house church we attended while at

MRAP), and our supporting churches, I am virtually certainly that we would not be in missions. I am not even sure we would be in ministry today. As one family counselor put it, we had been wounded by shame but healed by grace.

CHAPTER 16

Finishing in Bicol and Beginning at APTS

After finishing our year at MRAP, we still needed another year at home to raise the prayer and financial support that we needed to return for our fourth term. By the time we returned to the Philippines on September 30, 2011, we had been gone over two years. When the date of our return was certain, I had Alan start looking for a house in the same subdivision in Daraga where we had always lived. The place he found was kitty-corner to the first house we had rented, and it turned out to be our favorite of the three houses we lived in during our years in Bicol.

Like the others, this house had a large room that we could use for an office. The house also had several bedrooms, one of which we turned into a den where we put an air-conditioner and our TV, along with our easy chairs and reading lamps. This, rather than the living room, became our place to relax in the evening. This house had an American style walkout basement, the only basement I have ever seen in the Philippines. I had started weightlifting during our time at MRAP. I bought my own weightlifting equipment in Manila as soon as we returned and brought it down to Bicol. The main room in the basement was ideal as a weight room, so I set everything up down there.

This house came with an extra lot, and the person who built that house had constructed a small, one hoop, paved basketball court on that lot, much to my delight. Later, we got permission from the landlord, and one of my team members, Ronald, who was a licensed basketball referee, drew a three-point line, a free throw lane and a key. We also installed extra lighting for the court in a nearby tree. To make things more fun, an electric wire hung high over part of the court as did a branch or two of the tree. We declared that these things were "in play," and that if that ball hit them, we would not call interference. Within days of our arrival, we picked up Sam from the friends who had faithfully cared for him for much longer than they had expected. We declared that if he trotted across the court and got hit with the ball while we were playing, he, too, was in play. Fortunately for him, Sam was not a basketball dog and usually stayed far away when we played. We had many, many hours of fun and laughter on that court.

We also shared the property with our landlady's maid and her family, who lived in a small house on the backside of the property. The maid's husband served as the caretaker of the yard. We had many hours of fun playing with their children, the eldest of whom later died of leukemia after we moved to Baguio. The kids loved Sam, who was always wanting someone to give him attention.

Alan had led the team well, and that part of transitioning back was easy. When we left in 2009, Debbie had already agreed to keep teaching at EBC when we returned, even though she was no longer president. After we returned, we discovered that they had enough faculty and she was not needed. While this was hard for her, she accepted it with her usual grace and love. In looking back now, I think the Lord was preparing us for the unexpected change that was coming.

While we were in Manila before heading back to Legaspi, we met with our area director, Bill Snider, to get an update on what was happening on the field, and to let him know what we thought the coming term would look like. Bill asked if we would consider one of a couple of other possible part-time ministries outside of the Bicol region. First, he said that APTS had asked permission to talk to us about teaching part-time on a regular basis on campus. They wanted us to teach two courses apiece every year, which would not require that we move to Baguio. We could teach two- to three-week block courses once or twice a year. He also stated that they also wanted at least me to be involved in publishing their academic journal, the *Asian Journal of Pentecostal Studies* (*AJPS*). The other option was to consider conducting pastors conferences in other districts. Since we had just returned, we asked him if we could delay a decision on these matters until we got settled back in Bicol, and he agreed. We honestly put the whole discussion out of our minds for six months. Getting settled and back to work after being gone so long commanded all of our time and attention.

Six months later, in February 2012, we went to Manila for some field in-service training, and Bill inquired again if we would be willing to consider these requests. We agreed to give it serious prayer, and about a week or so later, we emailed Bill that we would be glad to talk to APTS. Shortly afterward, we were contacted by Kay Fountain, an AG missionary from New Zealand who had become the academic dean. She clarified that they wanted me to become the new managing editor of the *Journal* and that Debbie would serve as one of the editors. These assignments were in addition to the teaching assignments they were requesting. After more prayer and discussion, we believed that the Lord was in it, and we accepted her invitation.

By this time, we had not been on campus for a few years, so we decided to go in June, following the AGMF annual meeting, just to visit and learn about our new jobs. We spent a lot of time meeting with Kay. We also met Juliet Pascual, the faculty secretary, who would also serve as a part-time secretary for the *Journal* and APTS Press, although the Press was not added to my portfolio until later. Putting our teaching schedule together was relatively easy. Debbie would teach English and I would teach a course called Pentecostal Ministry in Animistic Contexts, plus one other course that would be determined at a later date.

Most of my time that June was spent learning about, and getting started on, the *Journal*. The *Journal* began in 1998 under the leadership of APTS chancellor, Bill Menzies, and his assistant, Wonsuk Ma, the academic dean at that time. The purpose of the *Journal* was to give Pentecostal scholars in Asia an opportunity to reflect on the issues of the day. It was published serially twice a year. They had a small subscription list, and they participated in a journal exchange with over sixty other theological institutions from various Christian traditions that published journals. This gave the *AJPS* a wider distribution and the APTS library benefitted from having more journals available.

The *Journal* was published regularly until at least 2007. After they left, it fell into a period of difficulty and was not published for at least four years. Paul Lewis, Kay's immediate predecessor as the academic dean, made a valiant attempt to get the *Journal* caught up and up-to-date before he left in March 2012. He published several editions. When I came onboard a few months later, the *Journal* was still a year and a half behind in publication. Kay and I set a goal to publish five editions of the *Journal* in the next eighteen months. Since I had never edited a journal before, and because we only had enough articles for one edition on hand, it was an ambitious goal.

Somewhere along the line, Kay also agreed to publish my doctoral dissertation through APTS Press, which had long been my dream. After this, Kay revealed that no one was currently overseeing the Press, and she hinted that this position might be open to me if I were interested. I had no such plan, but the Holy Spirit began to deal with me. In September 2012 I also became the director of the Press, even though we were still living in Bicol.

My seminary studies at AGTS back in the 1980s had helped me to understand that biblically authentic theology is always done in a social and religious context. Most written theological reflection in the last several hundred years has been done in the West, especially in Europe and the United States. Since the questions people bring to the study of the Bible are drawn from their life experience in their context, many questions that Asians had were not answered in theological books written by western scholars that have never lived in Asia.

When I came to the Philippines in 1994, I had a desire to participate in discussions on Asian theological and missiological issues. I wanted to write articles and books that dealt with these issues, once I had been in Asia long enough to know what the issues were. I never dreamed at the time that I would be given the opportunity to oversee the publication of an academic journal or direct a book publishing ministry. But by the time these opportunities did come my way and I understood at least some of the Asian issues, God had prepared me through leading the *Full Life Study Bible* projects in Tagalog and Cebuano, as well as publishing my first book, so I did have some understanding of the publishing process. I attacked the work with gusto and we got the *Journal* up-to-date in fourteen months instead of eighteen. We also published my dissertation five months after I became the director of the Press.

About the time that I became the director of the Press, the Cebuano *FLSB* was finished, after four years of hard work. Finally, in late 2012, we were able to start marketing it. We scheduled two launches, one in Cebu and the other in Davao, the largest city in Mindanao. Debbie and I flew to Cebu, arriving about the same time as the PBS leadership, so we shared a van ride to the hotel where the launch ceremony would be held. By this time, Debbie and I had become good friends with the PBS leaders. While en route to the meeting, Nora Lucero, the General Secretary of the PBS, turned to me, and perhaps half-jokingly, said, "Well, Dave, what's next? Ilokano?" This was the dominant language of the northern Philippines. My answer, and the result of that discussion will be taken up in the next chapter.

Meanwhile, life went on in Bicol. While Debbie no longer taught at the Bible school, she did continue to direct the Church Planting School Program (see chapter 13). Things began to change after we left for itineration in 2009. Some people lost interest in keeping their programs going and one key leader became terminally ill. By the time we returned in 2011, 206 house churches had been planted. However, only a couple of the church planting schools were still functioning. Many of the house churches had been absorbed into the mother church, and some had become more traditional churches themselves. Also, in April 2012, the BRDCAG pastors elected a new superintendent, whose vision for church planting was different from the model we were using. He had no objection to our continuing the program and there was no conflict, but we have always tried to support the vision of the Filipino leadership.

The Frenches were still involved with the Church Planting School program (CPS). I joined the team in an effort to better support Debbie's ministry initiatives, and because my other responsibilities were less demanding. This time, we focused on adding a new level of training, which we called CPS II, and focused more on church strengthening. We covered subjects such as mentoring, conflict resolution, leadership, goal setting, communication and other similar subjects. Nevertheless, CPS II never took off as well as CPS I had, and died of natural causes after we moved to Baguio.

One of the reasons we could take on responsibilities at APTS while maintaining the lessons that we had learned at MRAP, was because neither the Cebuano *FLSB* project nor CPS II were all that time-consuming for me. However, another reason that gave us more time was becoming apparent. Although Alan had done a great job of leading the team in our absence, not all was well with the evangelistic ministry. As time went on, the number of invitations we received for outreaches began to diminish significantly. Part of the reason can be attributed to the fact that we no longer purchased Bibles and New Testaments for follow-up in our outreaches. Part of the reason for this was a more restricted budget, but another reason was that we felt it was time for the churches to pick up the financial burden instead of us. Apparently, the pastors thought differently. For the most part, however, we did not understand what was going on, and we were rather hurt. To the best of our knowledge, then and now, there were no relational issues or tension with the pastors. Even Alan did not understand what was happening. Looking back now, I believe that God was closing the doors. Had we continued to have a robust evangelistic schedule I might not have heard the voice of God calling us to APTS.

Debbie was already hearing the Holy Spirit speaking to her heart. When we had visited APTS in June 2012, they invited us to consider coming full-time. She even began to have dreams about us moving there. When my beloved doberman, Sam, died of a heart attack in my presence in November 2012, she was sure that this was a sign from God because she thought there was no room for him at APTS. She knew that I would never part with him willingly. I had a different perspective on Sam's death, and I did not appreciate her interpretation of that event. I also did not see us going to APTS full-time. Evangelists normally do not teach full-time in seminaries, and I still felt called to the evangelistic ministry. I had been serving in the evangelistic ministry since I started traveling on weekends back in my seminary days in Springfield. What I did not realize was that God was lifting the mantle of the evangelist from me. God was giving me the mantle of a teacher and mentor instead.

Debbie and I had a number of discussions on these issues. I was open to going to APTS full-time, but I just did not see it happening. Then, we went there in February 2013, for Debbie to teach a block course, and everything changed. I accompanied Debbie to Baguio with the intention of working with Juliet on the *Journal* and Press and maybe do some research in the library. Then I got a call from Alan saying that some possible speaking invitations in Bicol had fallen through, which I found disappointing. As soon as I hung up, God spoke to me and said "Dave, you are done in Bicol, and APTS is the next move!" I also had a strong sense of urgency. After getting approval from Bill Snider, I called Kay and said, "If you still want us to come full-time, we're ready to talk." We met her and the president, Tham Wan Yee, a Malaysian AG missionary, the next day.

Two months later, we were packing and moving to Baguio. In the intervening months we took a lot of time to say goodbye to our many friends and colleagues in Bicol. I cried when I told Alan we were moving.

We had become close during the seventeen years we worked together and I felt like I was losing my right arm. Once we had said our goodbyes, we hired a vegetable truck to carry our things to Baguio—and that is not a "Veggie Tale!" Debbie went by plane to Manila and then by bus to Baguio a day before we left. The next day, I flew to Manila while Alan and one of the other guys drove our truck and someone else went with the vegetable truck. I met the guys in Manila and drove us on to Baguio and we arrived at APTS 3 a.m. May 1, 2013.

APTS is an international community with students from twenty-five to thirty countries in any given trimester. The faculty comes from eight or nine different nations. Nearly all the students and all the resident faculty lived right on campus, which contributed to the international flavor of the school. For the most part, it can be an enriching experience, but because we all come from other cultures, it can be challenging. The close proximity also meant that people could see the weaknesses in our character because there was no place to hide. Our house, situated right across the drive from the main academic building, was the back half of a duplex. It had two bedrooms upstairs, one of which we converted into a home office/library. The house also had a kitchen, dining room and living room downstairs. Debbie hired a wonderful charismatic Catholic named Irene Lunar to be our domestic helper.

Since the school year runs from June to March, the summer programs were in session when we arrived, but most of the students and faculty were not on campus. This meant that we had time to settle in before things got too hectic, although Debbie, as the new head of the English Language Program, did not have as much time as I did. By the time June rolled around, we were pretty much ready to go.

English is the most popular second language in Asia, especially in the academic community. Most of our textbooks and books in the library came from the West, making English the natural language of instruction at APTS. Debbie, who has always been an innovator never satisfied with the status quo, set about renovating the entire program. Her predecessor, who departed about a month after we arrived, had a good program. Nevertheless, Debbie felt that the program needed to be geared more toward learning the theological terms and concepts that the students would encounter in their classes. All students had to take a four-hour English test every trimester until they achieved a certain score before they could enter the degree programs. Debbie thought it might be better to allow advanced English students to take one or two regular courses while still taking some English courses. Then, they could be gradually integrated into the regular programs. She also asked the faculty if some of the English students could just sit in regular classes without taking them for credit. Then, they would move back to their own classroom to discuss what had been taught with their English teacher, who also attended the class. The faculty gladly agreed to give it a try. These experiments worked well and soon became official policy.

I think I could have done a decent job of handling the publishing ministries while living in Bicol. But I quickly noticed that if I wanted to do a great job, our move to Baguio was critical. This allowed me to invest much more time and energy in the work now that it was my primary ministry. It also put me in close proximity to the people with whom I was working, especially Juliet.

For the first time in thirty years of ministry, I now had an office outside of our home, and I loved it. A home office had a number of advantages, but having one in the faculty office complex gave me more interaction with the students and other faculty members. It also gave me a change of scenery. The office I eventually came to occupy had a stunning view of the Cordillera mountains that surrounded Baguio.

In addition to publishing, Kay also asked me to coordinate the Master of Theology program, which is one of the three postgraduate programs that APTS offers. This made me a member of the postgraduate committee. This took some adjustment because in the thirteen years in Bicol, we never had a committee for anything! If we wanted something done, we just went out and did it, or hired someone to do it. I am generally of the opinion that God so loved the world that he did not appoint a committee! Eventually, I began to see the value and strength of working together. It became a joy to work with the other committee members, even if they did not always agree with me!

By the time we had moved to APTS, we were well on the way to getting the *Journal* caught up. I then turned to the business side of the *Journal,* and I discovered that it was deeply in debt to the APTS general fund. Part of the reason for this was that we had overprinted the number of copies of previous editions. By the time I could begin to address the issue, there were over 11,000 copies of old journals gathering dust in our storeroom. I was able to raise some funds to help to continue publish the *Journal.* I worked with the administration to deal with the debt, but it took at least a year or two to get the *Journal* on sound financial footing.

Journals just sitting in storage do not help anyone. We were able to sell some of them at discounted rates, but we did not sell them as fast as I had hoped. In early 2017, I got permission from Kay to just give them away to whoever wanted them. We began emptying our storeroom, getting these great publications into the hands of people who could use them. We were also in a position to decide the themes for our journals, anywhere from six to twelve months in advance. This enhanced the quality of the *Journal* in the future.

Once we began to get caught up on the *Journal,* I started giving more attention to the Press. As mentioned above, the published version of my dissertation was already in process and came out in January 2013, shortly before we moved to Baguio. It was the first book published by APTS Press since 2006. The editorial guidelines were thirteen years old, and there was nothing even closely resembling an operations or policy manual. Additionally, there had never been a marketing plan, except for selling books in the campus bookstore. Kay described it well when she said the Press was little more than "a rusty, old logo with a few books published in the past."

In fairness, the revolution in digital publishing and marketing has taken place only in the last fifteen years or so, meaning that I had more marketing opportunities than previous directors had. Up until 2006, they had done well with producing some good books and marketing them where they could. One book had even been translated into Spanish, and Global University in Springfield MO was using it all over Latin America. In contrast to the *Journal*, the Press had some money in the bank that I put to good use. I took the situation I was given as an opportunity to reinvent the Press, and the APTS leadership backed me all the way.

My first task was to find more manuscripts to publish and get the ball rolling again. Kay asked that I focus on publishing theses and dissertations, reflecting the academic DNA of APTS. I knew that Russ Turney, our AGWM regional director, had just completed his Doctor of Ministry dissertation on missionary longevity at APTS. I read it and thought it would be publishable if we made some alterations to appeal to a broader audience. Russ was amenable to those changes. We had it ready by July 2013, and we were able to launch it at an Asia Pacific gathering of missionaries in Chiang Mai, Thailand, that month. We also had it available at the triennial Pentecostal World Fellowship meeting in Kuala Lumpur, Malaysia, the following month. We finished 2013 feeling like we were moving forward. With this book, we started making the theses and dissertations we published a part of a new series of books that we called the *APTS Press Monograph Series*. We labeled my book as the first book, and Russ's became the second.

In 2014 Frank McNelis joined the editorial team. He was an American married to a Filipina living in Baguio. They were pioneering a church affiliated with the Foursquare Church, a Pentecostal denomination from the United States. He graduated from APTS in 2013. He was a diligent and dependable editor, as well as a walking encyclopedia of the formatting style used by APTS and the Press and *Journal*. He was so good that we eventually named him as the senior editor of the whole team. I came to heavily rely on him, becoming good friends along the way.

I really pushed us hard to publish as many books as possible in 2014 in order to test our maximum capabilities. In the end, we got three new books out, making five books in two years. The first book we published that year was entitled, *Understanding the Iglesia ni Cristo* (Church of Christ)*: What They Really Believe and How We Can Reach Them* by Anne Harper, an evangelical missionary who lived in Manila. The *Iglesia ni Cristo*, not to be confused with the American denomination called the Church of Christ, is a large indigenous cult group in the Philippines. They deny the deity of Christ, among other things, and have a strong influence in Filipino society. This became the third book in our *APTS Press Monograph Series*.

The next book was called a *Festschrift*, a type of publication unique to academia. This is a book of essays done in honor of a faculty member, or members, who have distinguished themselves in their fields over a long period of time. The theme of the *Festschrift* is normally along the lines of a subject important to the honorees. In this case, we chose to honor former Korean faculty members, Wonsuk and Julie Ma, who had served APTS for over twenty years. By this time, they were serving at the Oxford Centre for Mission Studies in the United Kingdom. The book was entitled, *A Theology of the Spirit in Doctrine and Demonstration: Essays in Honor of Wonsuk and Julie Ma.*

Several years earlier, the Press had started a series of books called *Pentecost Around the World.* The final book we published in 2014 became the fourth book in this series, and was entitled, *Pentecostal Pioneer: The Life and Legacy of Rudy Esperanza and the Early Years of the Assemblies of God in the Philippines,* by Rose Engcoy. Rose was one of our adjunct faculty members, and we launched her book in December of that year.

When I first became director of the Press, a friend with a publishing background encouraged me to focus on one market first in order to learn marketing well, instead of trying to take on the whole world at once. I took what he said to heart. The Philippines was a natural choice, since APTS was located there. Also, we had manuscripts about the Philippines available, and I had been scouring the local bookstores for years, so I already had some knowledge of that market.

When we were ready to expand globally, we began to work with a company called Flipside Digital Content to get our books out in eBook and mobile phone formats on retail online sellers such as Amazon.com. A few years would pass before we were able to support this with an international marketing program, but it was a small step in the right direction, even though sales were dismal in the beginning.

By late 2014, the workload had grown well beyond the time that Juliet could give to help me, and I got permission to hire a part-time marketing assistant. I hired a fine lady, and she really helped with the marketing. But after completing her initial five and a half month contract in 2015, she decided to resign and pursue other opportunities elsewhere. This change came only about two months before our next furlough in May 2015, so I did not have time to look for, and train, a replacement. This, combined with our need to focus on visiting our supporting churches in the States, meant that we lost a lot of the momentum that we had built up. Yet, we had laid a solid foundation that would still be in place when we returned.

CHAPTER 17

A Full Term at APTS

The first months of itineration in 2015 were unremarkable with one exception. I had the chance to take Debbie to San Diego. San Diego is the city where I had been baptized in the Holy Spirit, called into the ministry, and directed into the Assemblies of God so many years before (see Chapter 3). By this time, the Navy had closed the base that I had been on and they had turned it over to private enterprise. Many restaurants and shops had been opened on the old base and I took Debbie to see it. I also wanted to see if I could find the sidewalk where I had been walking back in 1976 when God called me to the ministry. We found it pretty easily, but I was totally unprepared for what happened next. Suddenly, I was overcome with a great sense of gratitude for all that God had done in and through me in the intervening thirty-nine years. It was overwhelming. Later, I took her past the old building that had housed First Assembly of God back then. This was the first AG church I had ever attended. I was baptized in the Holy Spirit in the basement of that church. The sidewalk where God had called me to the ministry was just another hunk of cement to others. But to me, it was holy ground. The church I attended was probably not much different than any other Pentecostal church of that time. But these places and these events are part of my spiritual heritage, which I deeply treasure.

If most of our itineration in 2015 was not noteworthy, 2016 proved to be another story. In February, Debbie was diagnosed with cancer, again, in the same breast where she had had it in 1999. This time, radiation and chemo were not an option, and she had to have a unilateral mastectomy. We cried buckets of tears, but God and friends helped pull us through, and we managed to keep moving forward. A bit of humor helped too. After surgery, one of the doctors quipped that they would keep Debbie in the hospital for only one night so that she did not have to eat much hospital food. I replied, "If that's the case, you'd better keep her here, because the other option is my cooking!" And cook I did! I cooked under Debbie's direction, usually given while she rested in the living room or bedroom. The food came out fine and she applauded my culinary efforts.

In July, we had just returned from a five-week road trip, and Debbie was scheduled to have the second part of breast reconstruction surgery. We had been home for less than an hour when we received word that Debbie's mom was losing her battle with Alzheimer's. By this time, Debbie's mom no longer recognized anyone. She seldom said a word to anyone other than her caregiver—and even then, only rarely. We had last seen her about seven months before, when we went to Washington State for the holidays. Every time we had seen her over the last few years, we had, in effect, said goodbye.

For these reasons, Debbie felt that it was more important to be there in time for the funeral, instead of rushing there to see her mom for the last time before she died. Debbie decided to do this, as we did not know how much longer Mom was going to live, and we wanted to be sure to be there for the funeral. Airline tickets in the States are notoriously difficult to change, and more importantly, she wanted to be there for her family members. And Debbie wanted to help her dad get started on life without his wife of nearly sixty-two years.

Mom passed away on July 20th and we flew out as soon as we got the news. The irony of this for us was that the funeral was held on July 26th, our 19th wedding anniversary and Debbie's birthday. We gathered in Debbie's home church, the same church where we had been married. To top it off, the minister who officiated for the funeral, Jack Rozell from

MRAP, was also one of the ministers who officiated at our wedding! We could see this date conflict coming, but there was not much choice. Two of Debbie's brothers lived out of state and had to work around other responsibilities. We chose not to let it bother us, but Debbie's brothers apologized profusely for having the funeral on our special day and her birthday.

As sad as we were, the funeral was a celebration of Mom's life and faith. Many, including me, told stories about how she had touched our lives. We rejoiced that she had lived for Jesus and was now with the Lord, free from disease and pain. Debbie's dad bore his sorrow well. Since the live-in caregiver, who had actually taken care of both of them, was no longer needed for Mom, we needed to move Dad, who was 89, right away. Debbie stayed an extra week to help Dad get settled into an adult retirement center, where he immediately put the word out to all the widows that he was not available!

The week her mother died, Debbie had been scheduled for outpatient surgery to finish plastic surgery reconstruction of her breast, which the doctors had started right after the mastectomy. We had to reschedule it for September, when we had hoped to be back in the Philippines. Since Debbie needed to see the doctor about six weeks after the final operation, and because we were still short of the funds we needed to raise, we remained in the States until after Christmas, which we spent with Debbie's family. We returned to the Philippines on December 28, 2016 to begin our fifth missionary term.

Despite the slowed momentum of the Press and *Journal*, we were able to continue publishing the *Journal* on time. We did get one book out while we were on itineration. We invited Alan to come up from Bicol and help us get resettled. While we were in the States, we had sublet our house on campus to another missionary couple. They had wanted to use some of their own furniture, so we put our things in storage on campus. This meant that we had to set up house again when we returned. The third trimester of the 2016-2017 school year was about to begin, and as head of the English Language Program, Debbie had to administer the English test and prepare for the trimester. So, Alan, Irene and I did most of the unpacking and household setup. This did not take long, and we soon sent Alan happily home.

No sooner had we gotten settled when Kay Fountain, the academic dean, who also pastored a small international church, announced that she was planning to retire after graduation in 2018. She asked us to join her church's leadership team to help through the upcoming transition. Joel Tejedo, one of our faculty members and an assistant pastor at the church, replaced Kay when she retired. We originally committed for only two years. At the end of that time, Joel requested that we remain on the team indefinitely, and we were happy to oblige, although I later resigned.

With itineration behind us, I could once again focus on the *Journal* and Press. After several frustrating months of being unable to find someone to work for me, I hired an APTS student, Carl Gaugano, as a part-time work-study student. We began to build momentum again. We also began to build an international email database for marketing the books we were selling through Amazon, and sales began to increase. We also convinced our online distributor, Flipside Digital Content, to start offering our books through print-on-demand, as well as eBook. Our print-on-demand sales quickly exceeded the sales of our eBook and mobile phone formats.

Carl worked for six months and I had to look for another assistant. After a few months of looking, I hired Hazel Chi, the wife of one of our students, to work thirty-five hours a week. We started moving forward once again. After a couple of months Hazel became pregnant and sick, consequently she had to cut back her hours. After six months, Hazel opted not to renew her contract because her husband was graduating and the baby was almost due. She had done a good job and helped in the growth and development of the Press. Then, I hired a man as a full-time employee, thinking that my challenges in finding long-term help were now resolved. But he lasted about ten days before he had to move on, because of issues not directly related to the Press.

Finally, in October 2018, I hired Steph Paderes, a twenty-year old Baguio native and university graduate with a degree in marketing. This was the first full-time job she had ever had. One of the reasons I hired her was because she had the courage of her convictions to respectfully disagree with me about our marketing strategy during the interviewing process. I like people who speak their minds! Throughout this entire time, Juliet gallantly helped fill in the gaps when I had no assistant and she was a real blessing. She continues to handle some of the Journal work for us.

Shortly after we arrived back from itineration, Kay asked me to represent APTS at a conference in Manila sponsored by the Asia Theological Association regarding creating and maintaining a good research culture on campus. While I was familiar with much of what was involved in a research culture, the actual term and concept were new to me. To put it simply, creating a culture of research means to create an attitude, atmosphere and resources where academic research can flourish. Learning all of this was part of my growing awareness that if we wanted to mentor Asian pastors through publishing books and journal articles that addressed theological and ministerial issues relevant to them, we also needed to develop a research culture where scholars could write on these issues.

Since having healthy postgraduate programs and publishing ministries are critical components of a research culture, I came to see my work in publishing and overseeing the MTh program (which included being part of the postgraduate committee that oversaw all of the postgraduate programs) as actually one job. The theses and dissertations being completed by APTS students are some of many excellent sources of potential manuscripts for future publication by the Press. For example, Russ Turney's book was the publication of his DMin thesis at APTS.

All this being said, however, the MTh program that I was overseeing was not growing, although most of the students in the program were making progress toward their degrees. In 2018 I became the supervisor of a thesis for the first time. This was a new experience for me, and I thoroughly enjoyed it. The student, Lora Timenia, was a junior faculty member. She completed her thesis on time and we published it following her graduation in 2020.

In early 2019, APTS was one a number of seminaries, mostly in the Majority World, that were invited by the Oxford Centre for Mission Studies (OCMS) in the UK to participate in building an online platform for mission studies. The goal would be to give Majority World scholars better access to such research. The APTS leadership was keen to accept the invitation, and I was asked to represent the school on this project. I was interested in doing so, but my workload was already getting heavy. I did not want to become a workaholic again, since I had learned my lesson in the past.

I agreed to accept this job if the leadership would agree to let me turn over the MTh program to someone else. One of our younger faculty members, Adrian Rosen, had served as the assistant coordinator of the MTh program while we were on itineration. He had done an excellent job. He and his family left for itineration a few months before we returned, and by early 2019 they were about to return. We offered him the position, and he gladly took over from me in April 2019, although I remained on the committee. Meanwhile, Debbie and I went to the UK for an organizational meeting at OCMS in February 2019. Along with representatives from at least fourteen other schools around the world, we began to develop the platform. At the time of this writing, the basic foundation is still being laid. There has not been any more work for me on this program yet.

From 2017 to 2020 we were able to publish ten new books. Further, we were able to put out a new edition of one book that we had published earlier. The *Journal* also kept rolling along and continued to be well received. During this time, we also worked to establish strategic licensing relationships with other publishers in other parts of the world. Our goal was to multiply the sales of our books through their networks. This would increase the reality that we have become a small but global publisher, giving us the opportunity to mentor more and more pastors and ministers all over Asia—and even to other parts of the world.

In the last chapter, Nora Lucero from PBS asked me if we were going to write the *Full Life Study Bible* in Ilokano. I discussed this with the AGWM, PGCAG and Life Publishers leadership. I also had a meeting with the PBS leaders, and together we decided that the Lord was, indeed, directing us to do this. We launched the project in June 2014, after giving Life Publishers time to raise at least some of the money needed for the project. We began with a week of translator selection and training. PBS took over from there, much like they had done with the Cebuano *FLSB*. Again, my role became minimal, and I stayed connected and helped resolve the inevitable problems that came along.

After the project was finished, the Bibles were printed in Korea and shipped to the Philippines. Then, we had a public launch in Baguio in December 2018, not far from the APTS campus. As usual, the leaders of Life and PBS came for the festive occasion, and we all had a great time together. The launch, as always, signified the completion of the translation and publishing, and inaugurated the marketing phase. While PBS was asked to do much of the marketing, APTS Press has played an active role, especially since the seminary is located in the heart of the Ilokano region. Anecdotal reports suggest that the Ilokano *FLSB*, the first study Bible ever published in that language, has been well received by the pastors and churches.

Shortly after we returned, APTS President Tham Wan Yee asked Debbie to take on the role of Dean of Students, in addition to heading up the English Language Program. After prayer and discussion, we felt that the Lord was leading in this direction. Debbie took on the job with her usual zest and zeal. She soon found out how big the job really is. In this job, she oversaw all student activities, including the work of the Student Council, and the making of APTS' annual yearbook, *The Chalice*. She assigned student housing, oversaw the chapel services three times a week, along with a multitude of other things related to the students' wellbeing. At times she has had an assistant Dean of Students, which has been helpful, as well as a fulltime staff assistant, but the workload was still heavy and she eventually relinquished the head of the ELP's job to someone else.

One of her greatest joys on this job has been simply interacting with the students. Between both of her leadership roles, she knows the names, backgrounds and dreams of nearly all of the students. Debbie regularly regales me with stories about what is happening with them, all without ever breaking anyone's confidence. Another one of her joys is the opportunity to do some student counseling and praying with the students. I have occasionally teased her about being one of the "mother superiors" of the campus.

We also did some travel. In 2017, I went to Malang, Indonesia, for the annual theological symposium of the Asia Theological Association. In 2018, the symposium was in Manila and I was able to present a paper on how cultural anthropology informs doing theology in Asia. This became the basis for an article that I published in the *Journal of Asian Evangelical Theology* in March 2020. In 2017, we made our inaugural visit to Cambodia to preach a missions' convention at the Cambodian Bible Institute of the AG in Phnom Penh. I returned to Cambodia later that year to attend the triannual General Assembly of the Asia Pacific Theological Association, where I was asked to become the vice-chairman of their theological commission. In 2018, we went to Chiang Mai in northern Thailand so I could attend a doctoral supervisors' seminar. Then we went on a wonderful three-day visit to Kunming in southwestern China for a consultation with some of our colleagues there. It was my first time in China since 1996, and Debbie's first time since she taught English for a year there in 1985.

In 2019, we both taught block courses at an AG school in Yangon, Myanmar. Later in the year, I taught a week-long course in Bhutan, a small Buddhist kingdom in the Himalayas where Christianity is legal, but believers are persecuted. It was our first time to be in these countries. In February 2020, I returned to Japan for the first time (except for passing through the airports) since 1977, when I was there with the Navy. This time I taught a block course at Central Bible College in Tokyo, the official AG Bible college in Japan. This course was the first in a joint partnership between APTS and the Japan Assemblies of God. In all of these places, except for China, I also preached in local churches. I greatly enjoyed the opportunity to learn more about Asia, and help extend the ministry of APTS and the Kingdom of God.

We both immensely enjoyed the social life on the APTS campus, either hanging out with our fellow faculty members or students over a meal, attending the many student-led activities, and the monthly faculty prayer meetings. Debbie often invites students over to chat; sometimes she even holds her classes in our living room. We have worked hard to cross the cultural and economic boundaries that exist in any school like ours. I think we have succeeded overall, but probably not perfectly.

Another of our great pleasures at APTS has been meeting new people that come from all over the world to teach or to speak for us. As much as possible, we try to have them over to our home for a meal or take them out to eat. We have made friends with some incredible people and our lives have been significantly enriched. We have become much better global citizens by learning so much from these friends.

I continued to enjoy sports. Nonetheless, I had to stop weightlifting and participating in basketball games when I was diagnosed with high blood pressure and an enlarged aortic valve in my heart. I had to limit myself to shooting baskets and walking, but I still enjoyed it. Debbie and I also enjoyed taking quarterly personal retreats at one of a couple of seaside resorts a couple of hours' drive down the mountains from Baguio. On two occasions in this last term, I have travelled to the States for mission business. I managed to spend a week or so each time with my family in Grand Rapids. Debbie accompanied me on one of those trips for a post-cancer checkup, and she stopped in Seattle to see her family for a few days on the way back. Thankfully, she remains cancer free.

As this book goes to press, we are completing our fifth missionary term. Although we are both in our sixties, we have no plans to slow down or retire anytime soon.

Epilogue

If I had to pick one word that expresses my feelings about all of the years of life and ministry that I have been blessed to have, I think that word would be "gratitude." I am so thankful for the life that God has given me, and the wonderful people, especially Debbie, with whom I have been able to spend that life.

As I mentioned in the introduction, I wrote this book out of a keen, Holy Spirit-directed desire to leave a legacy. One could certainly argue truthfully that most people leave a legacy without writing a book about it. In my case, however, I felt the Lord leading me to join a small legion of others over the last 2,000 years, who have felt led by the Lord to write their story. This book was an attempt to describe the people and events that have shaped my life. I also aimed to show how God used both the people and the events of my life to make me into the person I am. Perhaps, it also shows why he allowed me to do the things that I have done. I hope it all has been for the glory and honor of his name.

Whether I will leave a positive legacy is not mine to judge. For one thing, the legacy is not finished yet, because my journey has not yet ended. As I also mentioned in the beginning, writing this book does not mean that we have reached the end of the road. Whether Debbie or I will finish well has yet to be determined.

I am writing this epilogue in a time of great difficulty. Just a few weeks ago, one of our Asian faculty members died of pancreatic cancer. About three weeks later, Dwight Palmquist died of brain cancer in

Manila. He was the missionary who first invited me to the Philippines in 1983, the summer that changed my life. Dwight was also a close friend and colleague for all my years of missionary service. His cancer was diagnosed on a trip to the States, and at his request, he was allowed to return to the Philippines to die here.

That we are in the middle of the global COVID-19 pandemic compounded both of these sorrows. COVID-19 has resulted in severe restrictions on our movements, and public gatherings are prohibited, meaning that I was not able to be with Dwight when he died. We have been unable to hold any public memorial services honoring him, to help us grieve and move on. Yet, we find great hope in Jesus Christ. We have continued our ministries to the best of our abilities, knowing that there is a better day coming.

As this book goes to press in March, 2021, we are preparing yet another year of itineration in the States. Before returning to APTS to continue our labors there. We anticipate continuing in missions for several more years. When and if we do retire, we hope to remain in ministry somewhere, in some capacity, for the rest of our lives, doing our best to honor God's call. But even if that does not happen, we will remember that who we are is more important than what we do. Whatever form our future service to the Lord takes, we will continue to love and serve him as long as we live. Thank you for taking the journey with us.

Made in the USA
Monee, IL
26 July 2021